ALA BYE

HOW TO HANDLE TOXIC FRIENDS WITHOUT ENDING THE FRIENDSHIP

JOYDEEP GOGOI

Made with ♥ on the Notion Press Platform
www.notionpress.com

To Ala,
For the lessons, the laughter, and the love we shared. Though our paths may have diverged, the memories remain a cornerstone of who I am today.

To my friends,
Who stood by me, challenged me, and taught me the true meaning of connection and resilience. This book is a testament to the strength and complexity of the bonds we share.

And to the readers,
May you find a little piece of yourself in these pages and the courage to nurture the relationships that truly matter.

Contents

Foreword

Friendships are the silent architects of our lives, shaping who we are and how we navigate the world. In this book, the author masterfully explores the nuances of friendships—both enriching and challenging—with a voice that is equal parts candid and compassionate. What sets this work apart is its relatability; it doesn't just theorise relationships but draws deeply from personal experiences, inviting readers to reflect on their own connections. I believe this book will not only guide you in handling toxic friendships but also inspire a deeper appreciation for the bonds that truly matter.

Preface

This book was born out of my own journey through the labyrinth of friendships, particularly one transformative relationship that spanned nearly a decade. What started as a personal reflection soon evolved into a broader exploration of how we can navigate complex relationships without compromising our own well-being. I have drawn insights from both my own experiences and the wisdom of others, weaving them into a narrative that is as practical as it is heartfelt. It is my hope that this book serves as a companion for anyone seeking to maintain balance in their friendships, even when faced with toxicity.

Acknowledgements

This book would not have been possible without the unwavering support of my family and friends, who have been my sounding board and my greatest cheerleaders. To my former girlfriend, whose presence inspired this work: thank you for the lessons in love, respect, and boundaries. I am also deeply grateful to the countless authors and thinkers whose works have shaped my understanding of relationships, and to my readers, for trusting me to share this journey with you.

Prologue

Nine years ago, I met Ala—a relationship that would become both a blessing and a challenge, teaching me invaluable lessons about friendship, boundaries, and the delicate art of letting go. This book draws from that experience, offering insights into the complexities of human relationships. It is not a step-by-step guide, nor does it claim to have all the answers. Rather, it is an invitation to reflect, to question, and perhaps to see your own friendships in a new light. As you turn these pages, I hope you find the tools and the courage to nurture the relationships that uplift you and gracefully manage those that weigh you down.

Disclaimer

Just as real-life movies are categorised into three sections—

(a) Documentary: A documentary is a non-fiction film that explores a specific subject, often using interviews, archival footage, and on-location shooting to present factual information. An example is "Writing with Fire" (2021), an Indian documentary that follows the journey of a group of female journalists in Uttar Pradesh who run a newspaper, highlighting the challenges and triumphs of women in journalism in a male-dominated field.

(b) Real-Life Based: A real-life based story is a fictional narrative inspired by actual events or people. An example is "Shershaah" (2021), a biographical war drama based on the life of Captain Vikram Batra, a Param Vir Chakra awardee who fought valiantly in the Kargil War.

(c) Real-Life Inspired: A real-life inspired story is a fictional narrative that draws on real-life experiences or situations for inspiration, but does not necessarily adhere to factual accuracy. An example is "Gully Boy" (2019), a musical drama that draws inspiration from the lives of Indian street rappers, capturing the essence of their struggles, aspirations, and the realities of life in the urban slums.

The same way this book draws inspiration from my relationship with my former girlfriend. Names, places, and all identifying details have been changed to avoid any potential social media drama. However, the essence of the story remains true. This book is intended solely for informational and reflective purposes. The ideas, advice, and strategies outlined here are based on my personal experiences, beliefs, and interpretations of managing friendships, especially those that can be challenging or even toxic. Everything you read is subjective, shaped by what I've encountered in my own life, so these views might not apply to everyone.

Furthermore, the recommendations in this book are meant as suggestions, not as definitive solutions. You are responsible for considering your own circumstances, values, and boundaries when applying any ideas from this book. Neither I nor the publisher accepts any responsibility for actions taken or consequences arising from what you decide to do with the content provided here.

Ultimately, this book aims to inspire thought and reflection rather than provide absolute answers. So, thank you for reading, and please approach the content with an open mind. And the cover photo is an image I got from an agency. It's not someone I know personally. Don't bother searching her on social media. And yeah I've included a disclaimer—so I'm off the hook. Whatever you do, just make sure it works for you!

CHAPTER ONE

INTRODUCTION

As the legendary Bappi Lahiri so memorably said, "**Yaar bina chain kaha re**"—without friends, where is the peace, the joy, the fulfillment in life? It's a sentiment that resonates universally because friendships are, in many ways, the invisible threads that hold the tapestry of our lives together. They are not just companions on our journey but shapers of who we are, sculpting our personalities, perspectives, and even the way we navigate challenges. Life, with all its unpredictability and ups and downs, feels significantly less daunting when you have someone to share it with—a friend to laugh with, cry with, and simply exist alongside. Friendship gives life its richness, its flavor, and without it, the days can feel hollow, no matter how much else you have.

What's fascinating about friendships is how organic they often are. Unlike choosing a career path or planning a vacation, you rarely sit down and consciously decide, "Today, I'll make a lifelong friend." Friendships often sneak up on you. They happen in the corridors of your school, during late-night conversations in college hostels, or over shared coffee breaks at work. Sometimes, they come through serendipity—a mutual connection introduces you, and before you know it, you're inseparable. Other times, they come through shared circumstances, like being neighbors or teammates. What's remarkable is how these seemingly chance encounters can transform into bonds that define and enrich our lives for years, even decades.

And yet, what makes friendships so unique is the power of choice they bring. Unlike family—where you don't choose your parents, siblings, or extended relatives—friendships are a realm where you have agency. You can decide which friendships to nurture and invest in, and which to let fade. Life is too short to sustain every connection, so we naturally gravitate toward people who add value, who bring joy, and who align with our values and energy. Some friendships are effortless and feel like home; others require work but are worth every bit of effort because of what they bring to your life. The beautiful thing about friendships is that they evolve as we do—some people remain in your circle for a season, while others stay for a lifetime.

I've often thought about how universal this experience is. I've never met a single person who didn't have at least one friend, someone they could call their own. Even the most reserved or introverted among us find their tribe, their safe space, their people. Friendships remind us of our humanity. They teach us how to share, how to compromise, how to be vulnerable. They give us memories to cherish, stories to tell, and a sense of belonging that is irreplaceable. Life without friends is like a song without melody—it simply doesn't feel complete.

As I like to say, "**Babumoshai dost soch samajh ke banai nahi jati, ban jati hai.**" Friendships aren't something you plan—they happen, they evolve, and they grow. And that's what makes them so precious. I've realised that friendships are dynamic and multifaceted; they cannot be boxed into simple categories or defined by singular characteristics. Instead, they exist in many forms, shaped by context, circumstance, and mutual understanding.

That's why I like to think about the different types of friendships in what I call the BBSR Quadrant. It's my way of understanding the various dimensions that friendships can take on and how they evolve over time. This quadrant isn't about labeling people but about understanding where each friendship fits and how it contributes to the overall story of your life. Some friendships are built on emotional bonds, others on shared interests, and still others on deep, unspoken understanding. Each type, whether it's a connection made through shared hobbies or one that's forged through hard times, has a unique place in your life.

In this quadrant, the friendships that stand the test of time are those where you find a delicate balance. It's not always about being in constant contact or sharing every moment; it's about knowing that someone has your back, whether they're near or far. These are the friends who know you inside out, yet still choose to stand by you. They're the ones who don't need to be part of your everyday routine but are always there when it matters. They're the ones who have seen you at your best and at your worst, yet choose to stay, adapting and growing alongside you. It's this kind of friendship that brings depth and meaning to life.

Ultimately, the beauty of friendship lies not in its perfection but in its imperfection. No friendship is flawless, and no relationship is without its challenges. But it's through these moments of difficulty that we learn, grow, and come to appreciate the people who stick by us, no matter what. These friendships are not bound by time or circumstance; they are defined by the bond that exists between two people, built on trust, love, and understanding. And this, I believe, is what makes friendship one of the most profound and transformative experiences of life.

As I like to say, "Babumoshai dost soch samajh ke banai nahi jati, ban jati hai." I feel like categorising the types of bonds in BBSR Quadrant:

BBSR Qudrant(men perspective) - Buddies Brother Social Romantic

With BOYS:

1) ACTIVITY BUDDIES:

These are the friends you connect with over shared passions, activities, and hobbies. They're the ones who get just as excited as you do about last-minute hiking trips, weekend road adventures, or those late-night gaming marathons that stretch until sunrise. For some, they're the companions you meet at your favorite bar, where you unwind, have a laugh, and enjoy a few beers. For others, they're the teammates you play with on the sports field, whether it's football, basketball, or a casual weekend cricket match at the park. There's something truly special about the bond that forms during these shared moments—experiences that create lasting memories well after the activity ends.

These friends might not be the ones you lean on when you need emotional support, but they're the ones you can always count on for a good time. They're the ones who know all about your favorite football team, your highest score in that competitive game, or how seriously you take a friendly match. What sets these friendships apart is their simplicity—they don't require constant effort or heavy conversations. They're fueled by shared energy, enthusiasm, and mutual enjoyment, making them incredibly easy to maintain. Even if life gets busy or you don't see each other for a while, the bond remains strong, waiting to pick up where it left off the moment you reconnect.

2) LIFE-LONG BROTHERS:

These friends go beyond the typical label of "friend" and truly become like family. They are the ones who've seen you through the ups and downs, often from a very young age. Some of them are childhood buddies who've stuck around from those awkward, cringe-worthy moments to the more confident versions of yourself. Others are family friends who have grown up alongside you, celebrating holidays, birthdays, and all the significant milestones that shape your life. No matter how much time passes between conversations or how much life pulls you in different directions, these friendships remain solid. The bond doesn't fade; instead, it picks up right where it left off, as if no time has passed at all. They are the ones who know your family just as well as you do, who have shared countless experiences with you, and who become trusted confidants in the truest sense.

These "brothers" or "sisters" are there for you unconditionally. They're the ones you can rely on to help you move into a new house without hesitation, stand beside you on your wedding day with heartfelt joy, or be the first to cheer you on after an accomplishment. What makes these friendships so special is the history you've built together, one filled with shared moments of joy, hardship, laughter, and growth. Loyalty, trust, and a deep understanding of each other form the bedrock of these relationships, creating a bond that feels unbreakable and lasting.

With GIRLS:

1) SOCIAL COMPANIONS:

These friends are the ones who make life's social moments brighter and more memorable. With them, it's less about deep, serious conversations and more about sharing experiences that bring joy and laughter. Whether it's spontaneous weekend brunches, shopping trips that turn into mini adventures, or cozy dinner parties that go on till late, these are the people who show up when you want to make the most of your free time. They're the ones you call when you feel like checking out a new café or need someone to take photos with at that beautiful, hidden spot you discovered.

What makes these friendships even better is the easy, relaxed vibe they bring. These friends are always ready to listen—whether you're catching up on life, reminiscing about old memories, or venting about your day over coffee. They might not always give you the deepest advice, but they're great at making you feel heard and understood. These friendships are often fueled by shared interests and passions, like a love for food, fashion, or simply exploring new places together.

Over time, the shared moments and simple joys build trust and familiarity, and what starts as casual hangouts often turns into something deeper. These friends become a core part of your social life, filling your days with energy and a sense of connection. They remind you that life is about enjoying the little things, and their presence turns even ordinary moments into something special.

2) ROMANTIC PARTNERS:

Sometimes, a friendship evolves into something more, gradually transforming into a romantic connection. These friendships have a way of blurring the lines between simple companionship and deeper love, creating a bond that is both emotional and intimate. What begins as a connection based on shared interests and experiences gradually deepens into something more profound. You may start by simply enjoying each other's company, laughing together, and engaging in meaningful conversations, but as the connection grows, you realize that the comfort of friendship naturally merges with the intensity of romance.

This type of bond is rare and special because it's rooted in mutual respect and trust, built on the foundation of truly knowing and understanding one another. Your partner, who was once just a close friend, becomes not only someone you share your life with but also your confidante, your cheerleader, and your most steadfast supporter. What makes these relationships so unique is that they offer the best of both worlds. You get the ease of friendship—someone to laugh with, confide in, and rely on—combined with the passion and intimacy of a romantic partnership.

These friendships-turned-romantic relationships teach us important lessons about love, vulnerability, and companionship. They help us understand what it means to love selflessly, while also providing the kind of emotional support that makes life's challenges feel a little easier to face together. They're the kind of connections that last because they're built on deep, unwavering trust and affection.

During my engineering days, our college hosted an annual fest that stood out as one of the largest and most vibrant events in the entire region. It was always an event to look forward to—a massive celebration that attracted students from various colleges, all eager to witness the energy, excitement, and scale that made our fest so legendary. The atmosphere was electric, filled with people from all walks of life, each contributing to the collective buzz. It was during one such fest that I met Ala, a student from a different college, studying psychology. Her presence was magnetic; it was as if she carried a vibrant energy with her that effortlessly drew people in. She didn't just blend into the crowd—she stood out, and somehow, our paths crossed in the midst of that organized chaos.

We exchanged a few words, nothing more than pleasantries in passing, but something about her left an impression on me. After the event, I couldn't stop thinking about her. Thanks to the world of social media, specifically Facebook, I found her profile and, impulsively, sent her a friend request. I honestly wasn't expecting much, but what followed next changed the course of my life. We started talking—casual at first, but then late-night conversations became more frequent. Our chats eventually deepened, and before long, I found myself asking for her WhatsApp number. That simple exchange of contact details led to a whirlwind of texts, calls, and messages that eventually turned into a full-blown relationship. It wasn't long before we were calling ourselves boyfriend and girlfriend, a relationship that seemed almost too perfect for real life. It felt like something out of a movie.

The interesting part about our connection was how starkly different we were in almost every way. Ala was bold, outgoing, and loved to be the center of attention. She thrived in social settings—going to clubs, dancing to loud EDM music, meeting new people, and embracing every new experience with open arms. I, on the other hand, was the polar opposite. I was quiet, introverted, and preferred routine over spontaneity. My life was like a carefully designed system with early mornings, organized schedules, and very little room for unpredictability. Yet, it was precisely these differences that drew us together. Where she was free-spirited, I was structured; where I was predictable, she was adventurous. Despite our contrasting personalities, we somehow balanced each other out.

However, as time went on, those differences, which had initially seemed exciting, began to create friction. Over nine years together, we went through the full spectrum of emotions—joy, love, misunderstandings, disagreements, and eventually growth. One of the biggest challenges we faced was coming from two completely different backgrounds. Ala was from a big city, used to a fast-paced life, while I was from a small town, where the rhythms of life were slower, quieter, and more predictable. Our cultural backgrounds, upbringing, and even the way we viewed the world were worlds apart. But instead of letting these differences drive us apart, they pushed us to grow in ways we never imagined.

It was during this time that I realized how much Ala had taught me—especially about the importance of friendships. Before I met her, I hadn't really put much thought into the value of close relationships outside of family. Growing up in a small town, I never had to think much about forming a strong social circle. My focus was always on academics, discipline, and maintaining a rigid lifestyle. But Ala showed me how important it is to build meaningful relationships. She introduced me to the concept of boundaries, of knowing when to say "no" and how to protect my own well-being while still staying connected to the people I cared about. These lessons came from watching how she navigated her own friendships—how she effortlessly built a support system of friends who lifted her up, supported her dreams, and respected her boundaries.

Friendship, as I came to understand, is one of the most complex and profound aspects of life. It's woven into the fabric of our social existence, shaping who we are and how we experience the world. Jim Rohn once said, "We are the average of the five people we spend the most time with." In many ways, our friends shape our lives in ways we don't even fully realize. They influence our decisions, support us through difficult times, and push us to become better versions of ourselves. But not all friendships are the same. Some relationships are easy—uplifting, supportive, and fulfilling—but others can be more challenging or even draining. As Aristotle wisely said, "A friend to all is a friend to none." It's a reminder that we can't be everything to everyone, and true friendships require a discerning eye. Sometimes, we have to let go of relationships that don't serve us, and this is an essential part of growing as individuals.

Healthy friendships aren't always easy to come by, but they're essential for a happy, balanced life. True friendships are not about tolerating each other's faults without limits or avoiding disagreements. Rather, they're about mutual respect, trust, and growth. We have the power to choose which qualities we embrace in our friends, and which behaviors we need to avoid. Setting boundaries in a friendship isn't a rejection of the other person; it's a way of protecting our own mental and emotional well-being. It's a delicate balance to strike, but one that's necessary for lasting and meaningful relationships. Socrates once said, "Be slow to fall into friendship, but when thou art in, continue firm and constant." This quote embodies the essence of what I have learned about friendships. They require patience, understanding, and above all, the commitment to invest time and energy into nurturing them.

As I reflect on the friendships I've built, I realise that each one, whether fleeting or lifelong, has shaped me and taught me invaluable lessons about love, respect, and boundaries. This book is a collection of those experiences—a personal reflection on the complexities of human relationships. The most meaningful friendships are built on mutual understanding and respect, requiring effort but offering immense joy in return. They're about supporting each other through life's challenges and growing together, while staying true to ourselves and allowing others the same freedom.

In the end, friendships are not about perfect harmony. They are about understanding, compromise, and, most importantly, the willingness to grow. So here's to all the friends who have been a part of my journey—the ones who have stuck by me through thick and thin, and the ones who taught me the invaluable lessons that have helped me become the person I am today.

CHAPTER TWO

WHAT ARE FRIENDS?

DEFINITON of FRIEND or FRIENDSHIP

The concept of friendship has been an enduring part of human society for centuries, deeply woven into the fabric of our lives. From the earliest days of humanity, friendships have been a source of strength, joy, and support, whether in times of hardship or celebration. The importance of friendship has been recognized by many great thinkers, philosophers, and writers throughout history. Among them, Aristotle stands out, as he was one of the first to truly analyze the nature of friendship. In his work, Nicomachean Ethics, Aristotle classified friendships into three categories: friendships of utility, friendships of pleasure, and the highest form—friendships of virtue. The latter, as Aristotle explained, are built on mutual respect, shared values, and the genuine desire for each other's well-being. These friendships, he believed, were the most profound and enduring, and they laid the foundation for many of the ways we view friendship today.

When trying to define friendship in a way that resonates with modern experiences, it's tempting to stick with the dictionary definition: "a voluntary relationship between individuals who share mutual affection, trust, support, and common interests or experiences." While accurate, this definition feels somewhat sterile, as if it's stripping away the richness and emotional depth that make real friendships so special. Friendship is much more than a set of characteristics or a relationship built on mutual benefits—it is a living, breathing connection between people that is shaped by shared moments, mutual growth, and the rawness of human connection.

In my view, friendship is something much more personal and complex. It isn't merely a bond defined by shared interests or the need for support—it's about a deep, personal choice to invite someone into your life. Unlike family relationships, which we are born into, or professional connections, which often come with expectations and obligations, friendships are freely chosen. There is no compulsion, no duty; rather, it's the voluntary, genuine desire to spend time together, to learn from each other, and to support one another. The essence of friendship lies in this freedom—the ability to choose who we spend our time with, and why. In this sense, friendship is one of the most beautiful aspects of human life because it is entirely voluntary and based purely on connection.

What makes friendship particularly unique is the absence of societal expectations. Unlike family relationships, which can sometimes feel burdened by obligation, or romantic partnerships, which often come with demands and promises, friendships are grounded in mutual respect and affection. This makes them incredibly flexible. There's no rigid structure—no unspoken set of rules that governs what you must do for one another. You don't stick around because you have to; you do so because you want to. And when friends come together, it's often in moments of genuine joy and comfort—whether it's laughing together over an inside joke, venting about frustrations, or simply sitting in silence in each other's company.

A key element of strong friendships is the way they transcend time and distance. True friendships aren't measured by how often you see each other or how many texts you exchange. Rather, they are about the depth of connection that remains regardless of the passage of time. You could go months or even years without seeing each other, but when you finally reconnect, it feels like no time has passed at all. That's the beauty of a deep, emotional bond—it doesn't fray with time or get weakened by distance. It endures through life's ebbs and flows. The resilience of true friendship comes from its ability to survive the challenges of life—whether that means a change in location, different career paths, or new phases of life that create distance between you. The connection, however, remains strong, untouched by these changes.

Another defining feature of friendship is its adaptability. Unlike more rigid or transactional relationships, friendships can bend without breaking. They are flexible enough to evolve over time, adjusting to the different phases of life that friends go through. There's room for disagreement, for drifting apart for a while, and for coming back together without awkwardness. Friends are not bound by rigid expectations or scripts—they have the freedom to be imperfect and to change. In fact, many of the strongest friendships are those that weather conflict and are able to come out stronger on the other side. These friendships are resilient, able to adapt and evolve as both people grow and experience different aspects of life.

A true friend is someone who sees you at your best and at your worst and loves you for both. They are the ones who accept your quirks, who laugh with you in the best of times and stand by your side when things are tough. They are the ones who celebrate your victories as if they were their own, and who show up when you need them, not out of obligation, but because they want to. In many ways, friends act as mirrors, reflecting back to us the best versions of ourselves, reminding us of our worth, and helping us navigate the complexities of life. The true beauty of friendship lies in this support and unconditional acceptance—knowing that no matter what happens, there is someone who understands and accepts you as you are.

Friendship is often called a chosen family, and I believe this is a fitting description. While family ties are formed through birth and necessity, friendship is something we actively choose. We pick the people we want to walk through life with, and in doing so, we form a family of sorts—a group of people who are bound not by blood but by choice, shared experiences, and mutual affection. This makes friendships incredibly powerful. They are not shaped by the constraints of obligation or societal expectation, but rather by the deep connection that exists between two people who genuinely enjoy each other's company. There's something incredibly freeing about a friendship that is purely voluntary, grounded in trust and mutual respect, rather than any kind of imposed duty.

The beauty of friendship is that it transcends boundaries. It proves that sometimes, the relationships we choose can be even more significant than the ones we are born into. In friendships, we find a support system that is often as strong, if not stronger, than familial bonds. Friends are the people who stick by you through thick and thin, who celebrate your achievements and provide comfort during times of sorrow. They are the ones who lift you up, challenge you to be better, and make life a little more bearable simply by being there.

To sum it up, friendship is one of life's greatest gifts. It is the bond that is built on love, respect, and shared experiences, and it offers something that is often more lasting and more fulfilling than any other relationship in life. It's the foundation upon which we build our understanding of the world, of ourselves, and of others. Friendships remind us of the power of human connection and the deep sense of belonging that comes from being with people who truly care for us. It is a testament to the beauty of life—the way it becomes infinitely more meaningful when shared with others, and especially with those we choose to call our friends.

NOT EVERYONE IS A FRIEND

Friendship is a concept we often try to define, but the truth is, it can mean something different to everyone. The truth is, it can be hard to be upfront and honest about how we feel about certain people, especially when it comes to defining a relationship. We may hesitate to label someone as an "acquaintance" rather than a "friend" because we don't want to hurt their feelings or be perceived as dismissive. But the reality is, not every person we meet or interact with is a true friend, and it's perfectly okay to recognize that. There's no shame in labeling someone as an acquaintance, even if they are your benchmate, officemate, flatmate, or roommate. The key is to be honest with yourself. Ask yourself whether you genuinely enjoy their company and feel comfortable around them. Do you look forward to spending time with them, or do you feel drained, awkward, or disinterested? It's a simple yet profound question to ask, and it holds the key to understanding who truly deserves to be called your friend.

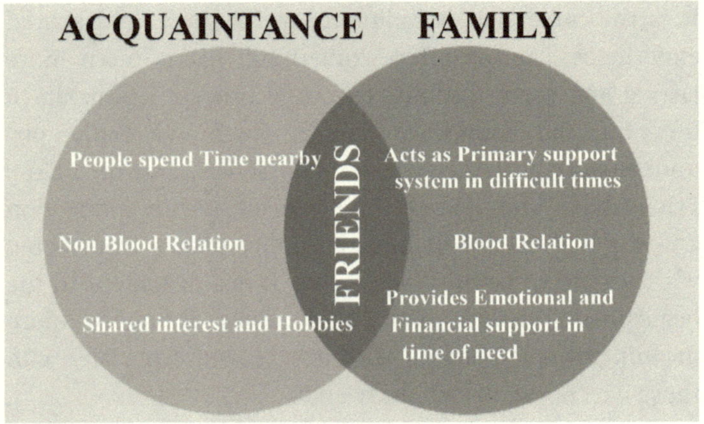

Family and Acquaintance Venn Diagram

In fact, C.S. Lewis, in his influential book '*The Four Loves*', explores the nature of friendship and suggests that not every acquaintance qualifies as a true friend. Published in 1960, Lewis delves into the concept of "Philia" or friendship, explaining that true friendship requires a deeper bond than just shared experiences or superficial interactions. He emphasizes that a real friend is someone who you share a common vision or interest with—a connection that goes beyond simple acquaintance or proximity. As Lewis points out, true friendship is rare, marked by mutual respect, understanding, and a unique bond that often develops over time.

Likewise, Aristotle, in his '*Nicomachean Ethics*' (published around 300 BCE), classifies friendships into three distinct categories: those based on utility, pleasure, and virtue. Each of these types of friendships has a different level of depth and longevity. Friendships of utility, for instance, are based on mutual benefit—like business partners or colleagues who interact because of the convenience and advantages it brings. Once the utility fades, so does the relationship. Friendships of pleasure are grounded in shared enjoyment or activities, such as socializing or engaging in hobbies together. While they can be meaningful, they are typically temporary and don't stand the test of time unless there's a deeper connection. The highest form of friendship, according to Aristotle, is the friendship of virtue, which is based on mutual respect, shared values, and a genuine love for one another that goes beyond what either person can gain from the other. These friendships are rare but are often the ones that last a lifetime because they are built on a solid foundation of trust, understanding, and goodwill.

While Aristotle and C.S. Lewis offer profound insights into the nature of true friendship, the reality is that our relationships with others don't always fit neatly into these philosophical categories. As we go through life, we often find ourselves in situations where we have acquaintances—people we interact with frequently, but who don't necessarily qualify as true friends. Whether it's your benchmate in school, an officemate, a flatmate, or even a long-time roommate, these are people you might spend time with regularly but don't share the same deep emotional connection that you would with a true friend.

But here's the thing: there's no shame in admitting that not everyone you know is a true friend. Being honest with yourself about who you truly connect with and who is simply an acquaintance helps you preserve emotional energy and invest in relationships that actually bring value to your life. The question you should ask yourself is simple yet profound: Do I feel happy and comfortable around this person? Do I enjoy spending time with them, whether it's during casual conversations, trips, dinners, or drinks? If your answer is no, it might be time to reconsider the label you give them. Friendship isn't something you should feel obligated to force. If the bond isn't there, calling it what it is—a friendly acquaintance—is the healthiest approach for both parties.

On the flip side, sometimes life surprises us. We might find ourselves forming an unexpected connection with someone we never thought we would. It could be someone from a completely different age group, culture, or background—none of those differences matter when you form a real bond. These are the friendships that defy all logic and expectations. They prove that friendship isn't about ticking off boxes or following a formula; it's about how you feel when you're around the other person. That's why it's so important to keep your heart and mind open to the possibility of new friendships, regardless of how unconventional they may seem. Friendship is unpredictable, and sometimes the most meaningful connections happen when you least expect them.

Ralph Waldo Emerson once said, "The only way to have a friend is to be one." It's a simple yet profound reminder that true friendship is a two-way street. You can't expect to have amazing friends if you're not willing to put in the effort yourself. Friendship is not just about having someone to hang out with or someone who laughs at your jokes—it's about being there for one another through thick and thin. It's about emotional investment, mutual respect, and the willingness to show up for each other when it matters most. True friends will be there for you when you're at your lowest, just as you'll be there for them when they need you. Friendship requires effort from both sides, but the rewards are immeasurable.

That being said, it's important to recognize that not everyone is naturally equipped to handle relationships in this way. I've encountered people who are so set in their ways that they refuse to compromise on anything. They'll say things like, "This is just who I am," as if that excuses their lack of consideration for others. While it's important to stay true to yourself, friendship is also about meeting people halfway. Relationships, whether they're with friends or partners, require flexibility and understanding. You can't always have things your way, and sometimes, the best friendships are built on the small compromises you make for the other person. It's about saying, "I care about what makes you happy," even if it means stepping outside of your comfort zone. Friendship isn't about being perfect; it's about being willing to show up, care for one another, and grow together.

Another common misconception about friendship is that you don't need friends to be happy. In today's world, it's easy to fall into the trap of thinking that being independent means being alone. Some people convince themselves that they don't have the time or emotional energy to invest in relationships, but the truth is, life is infinitely better when you have people to share it with. Helen Keller once said, "Walking with a friend in the dark is better than walking alone in the light." This quote captures the essence of friendship perfectly. Friends are the ones who provide support when things get tough, who make the darkest moments more bearable simply by being there. Even in the worst of times, friends can bring light into your life, offering solace, understanding, and encouragement.

Friendship is about quality, not quantity. It's not about how many people you know or how popular you are—it's about those few precious souls who truly make your life better. The friends who celebrate your victories as if they were their own, who support you when you're struggling, and who remind you that you're never truly alone—those are the friends who matter. It's not about filling your life with dozens of acquaintances; it's about nurturing the few relationships that truly enrich your life.

So, here's my advice: don't force yourself to call everyone a friend. Be honest with yourself about who adds value to your life, and don't be afraid to label some people as acquaintances instead. That doesn't mean you have to sever ties with them—it just means you're being real about the nature of your relationship. At the same time, don't close yourself off to new friendships. Stay open to new connections, even when they come from unexpected places. Keep your heart open, and remember that friendship can appear in the most unlikely of forms. Ultimately, friendship is one of life's greatest gifts—a reminder that no matter where we are in life, we're never truly alone.

HOW FRIENDS ARE MADE

The concept of using mathematical models, particularly the Random Graph Model, to understand friendships and social networks is a fascinating intersection of mathematics, probability theory, and human behavior. It offers a way to quantify and model relationships, providing insights into how we form bonds and how those bonds evolve over time. At the heart of this approach is graph theory, a branch of mathematics that deals with objects (nodes) and the connections (edges) between them. Graph theory allows us to study relationships in a structured way, applying mathematical principles to social phenomena like friendship. The introduction of the Erdős–Rényi Random Graph Model in 1959 by mathematicians Paul Erdős and Alfréd Rényi was a groundbreaking contribution in this field. Their work laid the foundation for understanding how random connections can form in large networks, and how, even within a random structure, patterns emerge that mirror real-life social networks.

In the Erdős–Rényi Random Graph Model, individuals are represented as "nodes," and the connections between them—friendships, in this case—are represented as "edges." The model assumes that each pair of nodes has a certain probability of forming a connection, which can be thought of as the likelihood of two people becoming friends. The simplicity of this model is one of its greatest strengths. It does not rely on any preconceived notions about how friendships form; instead, it assumes that the connections between individuals are random. However, as the network grows, patterns begin to emerge that resemble real-world social structures, such as clusters of friends or individuals who are more connected to certain groups. This randomness and the gradual emergence of structure make the model both powerful and versatile.

Despite its simplicity, the Random Graph Model acknowledges that some factors can increase the likelihood of connections forming between individuals. These factors are typically related to shared experiences or environments, such as living in the same dormitory, working at the same company, or attending the same school. Shared spaces create natural opportunities for people to interact and form connections, increasing the probability that they will become friends. These shared environments act as catalysts for friendships, making them more likely to form even in what might seem like random situations. The more frequent the encounters between individuals, the higher the likelihood that they will develop some form of connection. This aspect of the model provides a clear framework for understanding how relationships are often not purely random but are influenced by the contexts in which people meet.

However, while the Random Graph Model offers valuable insights into the structural aspects of social networks, it does not fully account for the complexities of human behavior and psychology that influence the formation and maintenance of friendships. This is where Social Exchange Theory comes into play. Developed in the mid-20th century, Social Exchange Theory offers a more psychological perspective on relationships, arguing that friendships and social bonds are not purely random but are driven by the principle of mutual benefit. According to this theory, people are motivated to enter and maintain relationships when they perceive that the benefits outweigh the costs. These benefits can take many forms, such as emotional support, intellectual stimulation, practical help, or simply companionship. Essentially, Social Exchange Theory suggests that friendships are formed when both individuals feel that they are gaining something valuable from the relationship, and that the relationship is worth maintaining.

For instance, consider two friends who meet in college. One might provide a listening ear and emotional support during difficult times, while the other introduces them to new experiences or offers fresh perspectives on life. Although they may come from different backgrounds, the friendship thrives because both individuals feel that they are gaining something valuable from the relationship. The balance of give and take is what makes the friendship sustainable. If one person feels that they are always giving and never receiving, the relationship can become strained and may eventually fade. Therefore, maintaining a healthy balance of benefits and costs is essential for the longevity of a friendship.

What is particularly interesting about Social Exchange Theory is that it acknowledges the dynamic nature of friendships. Friendships are not static; they evolve over time as circumstances, needs, and perceptions change. A friendship that begins based on shared hobbies or mutual interests might deepen into a more emotionally supportive relationship as one individual faces personal challenges. On the other hand, a friendship that was once strong can fade if one or both individuals feel that the relationship no longer offers the same level of value or fulfillment. This dynamic nature of friendships highlights the importance of communication, mutual respect, and understanding in maintaining meaningful connections.

The concept of shared environments, as emphasized by the Random Graph Model, also plays a role in Social Exchange Theory. In both frameworks, the frequency of interactions and shared experiences can increase the likelihood of forming friendships. However, the depth and longevity of those friendships often depend on the perceived mutual benefits that each person gains from the relationship. Just because two individuals meet regularly doesn't necessarily mean they will become close friends. The relationship must provide something meaningful to both individuals for it to thrive. If one person feels unfulfilled or unsupported, the bond may not last, even if the individuals continue to interact frequently.

When combining the insights from the Random Graph Model and Social Exchange Theory, we arrive at a more comprehensive understanding of how friendships and social networks are formed and maintained. The Random Graph Model provides a structural framework for understanding how connections form based on probabilities, while Social Exchange Theory adds a layer of psychological complexity by explaining the motivations behind those connections. Together, they offer a more nuanced view of friendships, highlighting the roles of both external factors, such as shared environments, and internal factors, such as mutual benefit and emotional fulfillment.

These theories also underscore the complexity of human relationships. Friendships are not simply about proximity or shared experiences; they are a dynamic interplay of chance encounters, shared environments, and the mutual desire to give and receive support. While external factors like geography or social circles play a significant role in the formation of friendships, the strength and longevity of those friendships are determined by the emotional connections and perceived benefits that both individuals gain from the relationship. Whether it's the randomness of meeting someone in class or the deliberate effort to maintain a bond over years, the beauty of friendship lies in its unpredictability and the profound impact it has on our lives.

In today's increasingly connected world, these theories are more relevant than ever. The advent of social media and digital technologies has greatly expanded the scope of our social networks, allowing us to connect with people from all over the globe. While this increase in connections is remarkable, the fundamental principles of friendship formation remain the same. We still form relationships based on the opportunities for interaction and the perceived value of those relationships. What has changed, however, is the scale at which these connections can occur. We no longer need to be in the same physical location to form bonds; we can connect with others through digital platforms that transcend geographical boundaries.

The explosion of online communities, from social media platforms to specialized forums, has created new opportunities for people to meet and form friendships. In many ways, these virtual spaces operate under the same principles as the physical environments discussed in the Random Graph Model. The more opportunities people have to interact, the greater the likelihood that they will form connections. However, just as with physical friendships, the strength of these virtual friendships depends on the perceived benefits of the relationship. If a person feels that they are gaining value from the connection—whether through emotional support, shared interests, or intellectual stimulation—they are more likely to maintain that relationship.

Understanding the balance between these factors—probability, environment, emotional fulfillment, and mutual benefit—can help us navigate our social lives more effectively. In a world where social networks are vast and diverse, it's easy to become overwhelmed by the sheer number of connections we have. However, by focusing on the relationships that offer the most value and fulfillment, we can ensure that our friendships are not only numerous but also meaningful. In the end, friendships are not just about the number of people we know or the frequency of our interactions. They are about the depth of the connection we share with others and the mutual support and understanding that sustain those bonds over time.

The beauty of friendship, as both the Random Graph Model and Social Exchange Theory demonstrate, lies in its complexity and unpredictability. Friendships are influenced by a variety of factors, including chance encounters, shared experiences, and the ongoing effort to maintain the relationship. While the formation of friendships may seem random at times, there is an underlying structure and set of dynamics that guide the process. Whether through physical proximity, online interactions, or shared interests, the bonds we form with others are shaped by a blend of chance, choice, and mutual benefit. Understanding these dynamics can help us build more meaningful and lasting friendships that enrich our lives.

Social Exchange Theory (SET) is one of the most widely referenced theories in the field of social psychology, particularly when it comes to understanding the dynamics of human relationships. It helps explain how and why people engage in different types of interactions, including friendships. At its core, the theory posits that relationships are formed and maintained based on a cost-benefit analysis, where people strive to maximize rewards and minimize costs. But how did this theory come to be, and who were the key figures behind its development?

John Thibaut and Harold Kelley (1959):

The foundation of Social Exchange Theory can be traced back to John Thibaut and Harold Kelley's work in 1959. In their influential book, The Social Psychology of Groups, they explored how individuals assess the rewards and costs involved in social exchanges, particularly within the context of relationships. Thibaut and Kelley suggested that people stay in relationships when the benefits they gain from them are greater than the perceived costs. They introduced the concept of the comparison level, which is an individual's personal standard for what they expect from a relationship based on past experiences and societal influences. If a relationship meets or exceeds this comparison level, it is considered satisfactory and likely to be maintained. Conversely, if the relationship falls short, individuals may choose to exit it or seek other alternatives that offer better rewards. Their pioneering work laid the groundwork for understanding how individuals evaluate relationships and the decisions they make regarding them.

George Homans (1961):

In 1961, George Homans further developed the principles of Social Exchange Theory in his book Social Behavior: Its Elementary Forms. Homans expanded on the original ideas of Thibaut and Kelley by arguing that individuals in all types of social interactions, not just romantic relationships or close friendships, engage in cost-benefit analyses. According to Homans, people are motivated by the desire to maximize rewards and minimize costs in their interactions with others. These rewards can be anything from emotional support to material benefits, while costs could involve time, effort, or emotional strain. Homans's work emphasized that the principle of maximizing rewards and minimizing costs applies universally, regardless of the nature of the relationship, making it relevant to understanding all forms of social behavior. In the context of friendships, this means that individuals are more likely to remain friends when the benefits of the relationship outweigh the costs, such as the emotional energy invested or time spent. His broader application of the theory across different social contexts contributed to its widespread influence.

Peter Blau (1964):

Peter Blau's contributions to Social Exchange Theory, particularly in his 1964 work Exchange and Power in Social Life, added a crucial dimension to understanding human relationships. He emphasised the role of power dynamics and social structures in shaping exchanges, offering insights into how these forces influence the balance of relationships. Blau proposed that friendships, like other social relationships, are often shaped by the distribution of power between individuals.

In his analysis, Blau explained that power imbalances can arise when one person is more reliant on the other—whether for emotional support, resources, or other forms of value. This dependency can subtly influence how the relationship evolves, with one party potentially holding more influence or control. Importantly, Blau expanded the scope of Social Exchange Theory by incorporating the concept of social networks. He highlighted that relationships do not exist in a vacuum; they are part of a broader web of interconnected exchanges.

This perspective shed light on why some friendships endure, while others falter under the weight of inequality. Resilient relationships, according to Blau, are often characterised by a fair distribution of benefits and mutual respect. In contrast, friendships marked by significant imbalances are more likely to experience tension or dissolve over time. Blau's work remains influential, providing a nuanced understanding of how power and interconnectedness shape the dynamics of human relationships, making his theories as relevant today as when they were first introduced.

The Simplicity of Friendship Dynamics:

Now, while Social Exchange Theory offers a comprehensive framework for understanding human interactions, it's not always the easiest theory to apply in real life, especially when it comes to understanding the complexities of friendships. In fact, despite the academic intricacies of the theory, friendships themselves often feel intuitive and natural. At their core, friendships are built on shared experiences, trust, and mutual respect—factors that don't always fit neatly into a cost-benefit analysis. But this doesn't mean that elements of Social Exchange Theory don't apply in practical, everyday friendship dynamics.

Reflecting on my own friendships, I began to notice certain commonalities that seemed to form the foundation of most of them, regardless of how different the individuals were. While these may not be groundbreaking discoveries backed by decades of psychological research, they offer an easy and relatable way to think about how friendships develop and why they endure.

I've boiled it down to three basic ingredients: proximity, routine, and shared interests. These are the factors that seem to play a significant role in initiating and nurturing friendships. Let's break each of them down and see how they come together to create a foundation for lasting bonds.

Proximity- The Foundation of Many Friendships:

Proximity is perhaps the most straightforward and obvious ingredient in the recipe of friendship. You're much more likely to become friends with someone who is physically close to you, whether it's because you see them at work, school, or even in your neighborhood. Proximity creates the opportunity for interaction. If you live next door to someone or sit next to them in class, the chances of forming a friendship are higher simply because you're both present in each other's daily lives. This was something I noticed in my own life—many of my friendships began because we were simply in the same place at the same time, repeatedly. You wouldn't be friends with someone who lives halfway across the world unless you met them through some common activity or shared platform, such as online gaming or social media. It's the law of chance—when you're physically around people enough, the probability of forming a bond increases.

Routine- The Glue That Holds Friendships Together:

Proximity might bring people together, but routine is what keeps them in each other's lives long enough for a friendship to form. This is where the idea of familiarity and comfort comes into play. Routine brings predictability, and with predictability comes a sense of comfort. You're more likely to build a lasting connection with someone you see regularly, whether it's because you both go to the same gym, grab coffee at the same cafe, or take the same train every day. These repeated interactions build familiarity, which is often the first step toward deeper connections. Over time, routine transforms into habit. You might find yourself texting a friend every night, or meeting up every weekend. These small but consistent acts of connection help strengthen the friendship, giving it the space to evolve from a casual acquaintance into something more meaningful.

Shared Interests- The Spark That Ignites Friendship:

The final ingredient in the friendship recipe is shared interests. While proximity and routine set the stage, it's shared interests that truly ignite the spark of friendship. It's one thing to see someone every day, but it's quite another to discover that you both love the same type of music, enjoy similar TV shows, or have common hobbies. Shared interests provide something to bond over—something to get excited about together. They give you a reason to keep talking, to keep hanging out. It's like finding a piece of yourself in someone else. And often, these shared interests don't appear right away. Sometimes, they emerge after months of casual conversations or shared activities. You might discover that you both enjoy hiking or that you share a love for a certain type of literature. These commonalities give you the foundation to create lasting memories, which, in turn, strengthen the friendship.

The Unpredictability of Friendships:

While proximity, routine, and shared interests lay the groundwork for friendships, the reality is that not every friendship fits perfectly into this model. Some people become close friends even if they don't share any common activities or interests. Others may drift apart despite having all three ingredients in common. Life has a way of throwing curveballs—people change, priorities shift, and circumstances evolve. Sometimes, friends grow apart because they no longer share the same routine or live in the same place. Other times, a friendship may not survive because the emotional connection or mutual understanding isn't strong enough to withstand external pressures.

But the beauty of friendship lies in its unpredictability. Not every friendship follows the same path, and not all of them last forever. Some friendships are brief but intense, while others may endure for a lifetime. But by understanding the basic ingredients that often contribute to friendship formation—proximity, routine, and shared interests—we gain a better appreciation for the bonds we create. Friendships may seem random, but when you look closely, you'll notice that they often start with simple, natural factors. And that's what makes them special—each friendship is a unique, unpredictable connection, shaped by its own set of circumstances.

So, the next time you think about the people in your life, take a moment to reflect on how those friendships began. Was it because of proximity? Did you meet them because you were in the same place at the same time? Or was it shared interests that brought you together? Friendships may seem like random occurrences, but when you look back, you'll see that there's always a reason they started—and that reason makes them even more meaningful. And maybe, just maybe, it's those simple, often unnoticed factors that make our friendships some of the most important connections in our lives.

To make the whole thing less theoretical and more practical, I've created a Venn Diagram that explains the friendzone in a simple manner.

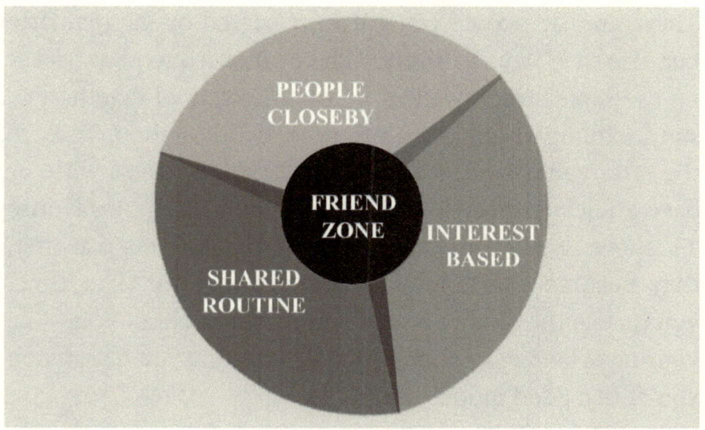

Fiend Zone Venn Diagram

1. PEOPLE CLOSE BY:

These are the friendships that almost seem to happen on their own, the ones that come into your life simply because of proximity or routine. You didn't actively go out and search for these people; life just brought them into your path. These friendships are often easy and low-maintenance because they're built on familiarity rather than grand gestures or shared ambitions. They feel like they're on social autopilot—you don't need to do much for them to exist, and sometimes, that's the beauty of it. The connections may start casually, but some of these people end up playing an unexpectedly big role in your life over time.

(a) Neighbourhood Friends:

These are the people you grew up around or see regularly because they're just... there. Maybe you used to play cricket on the same street, walked home from school together, or simply bumped into each other at the local shop. They're the ones you'd call for a quick game, share snacks with, or have endless conversations about school gossip or favorite TV shows. Even if the bond isn't particularly deep at first, they become a part of your everyday world. Over time, you realize they know a surprising amount about you—like your favorite flavor of ice cream or the song you hum when you're in a good mood.

These friendships often feel effortless because they're built into your routine. You don't have to go out of your way to spend time with them—they're already in the spaces you occupy. Whether it's borrowing notes, gossiping about the cranky neighbor, or spending lazy Sunday afternoons together, these friends make the everyday feel more connected.

(b) Family Friends and Cousins:

Then there are the friendships you didn't exactly choose, but they happened anyway. These are the bonds that stem from your parents' social circle or extended family. Maybe it's the kid of your dad's best friend, the cousin who lives just a town away, or the family friend who always ends up sitting next to you at weddings. At first, it might feel like these relationships are forced, like you're only hanging out because of circumstances. But something funny happens when you spend enough time together—you start to click.

You might bond over complaining about awkward family events or rolling your eyes at the same outdated traditions. Slowly, these "convenience" friendships can turn into real ones. The cousin you used to find annoying at family gatherings could become the person you call when you need advice. The kid of your mom's friend might become the one who helps you move into your first apartment or sends you random memes at midnight. What starts as an obligation sometimes evolves into something you genuinely treasure.

(c) Relocation or Geographical Friends:

Moving to a new city is daunting, and the loneliness can be overwhelming. That's when you tend to gravitate toward people in similar situations—those who are also figuring things out in the same unfamiliar environment. These could be your colleagues, roommates, or even someone you met in line at the local coffee shop. The shared experience of being "new" creates an instant connection.

At first, these friendships might seem temporary, like placeholders to help you get through the transition. You bond over the struggle of navigating a new place—finding the best grocery store, figuring out public transport, or learning which local spots are worth your time. But these shared struggles often build trust and camaraderie. Before you know it, these people are more than just your movie buddies or café partners; they're the ones who make the city feel like home.

What's beautiful about geographical friendships is how they're rooted in practicality but can blossom into something meaningful. These friends become your support system, helping you tackle the challenges of starting fresh in a new place. They're the ones who celebrate your small wins, like finding your favorite coffee blend, and help you laugh off the mishaps, like getting hopelessly lost on your first day out.

2. SHARED ROUTINE:

The next type of friendship often grows organically when you're regularly together in the same setting. It's not something you actively plan or consciously seek out; it just happens naturally over time because you're sharing similar routines day after day. The consistency of your interactions gradually lays the foundation for these connections. At first, you might just exchange pleasantries or share a few passing conversations, but before you know it, these small exchanges evolve into something more meaningful. It's the magic of spending time together consistently without forcing it. These friendships often start from the most ordinary moments and grow into some of the most valuable relationships you have. Here's how this dynamic plays out in various aspects of life:

(a) Roommates:

When you live with someone, you're in a unique position to witness their entire spectrum of personality—both their best and worst sides. The little things that you wouldn't usually know about someone start to become clear. The way they organize their stuff, their cooking habits, their choice of music, or how they deal with stressful situations. Living together creates this constant interaction, whether you're having late-night conversations, bickering over who forgot to take out the trash, or teaming up to handle the landlord's quirks.

The dynamics of roommate friendships are particularly interesting because they often start with practical necessity. At first, you're just two people sharing a space, trying to make the best out of the situation. But over time, those little moments—fighting over fridge space, celebrating tiny victories like making a really good meal together, or just laughing at each other's misadventures—build a bond that's hard to replicate. These relationships can become incredibly close because you end up seeing each other in your most vulnerable, relaxed moments. You may even form a partnership in tackling daily chores or hosting impromptu get-togethers.

However, not all roommate friendships last forever. Sometimes they're temporary, and the bond fades once you no longer share the same living space. But while it lasts, the friendship is real and meaningful because it's built on a foundation of shared experiences and proximity. Even if the relationship doesn't last, those memories of living together and navigating daily life will often remain with you for years.

(b) Project Group Members:

When you work together with people on a shared project, you experience a unique bonding opportunity. It's often a situation where you're all invested in the same goal, and you must rely on each other to get through challenges. Late-night brainstorming sessions, the pressure of meeting deadlines, endless cups of coffee to keep you going—it's in those moments of shared stress and struggle that bonds are created. What starts as a professional collaboration can often turn into a genuine friendship because you've been through the highs and lows of the project together. You know exactly what it's like to be in the trenches with those people.

It's remarkable how these group projects, which are essentially goal-oriented and work-driven, can lead to lasting personal connections. Those late nights spent problem-solving, the inside jokes that develop when you're under pressure, and the sense of relief when the project is finally completed are shared experiences that form the basis for friendship. What might have started as just a group of individuals with a common objective can often turn into a close-knit team where personal connections and support grow beyond the project itself. Even after the project ends, those group members might remain in touch, whether it's for social reasons, professional collaboration, or simply because you've shared something so significant together.

It's one of those friendships that wouldn't have existed if it weren't for the specific situation—working together toward a common goal—but once it has formed, it can be incredibly fulfilling. You understand each other's strengths and weaknesses, and there's a level of mutual respect and camaraderie that grows out of the shared struggle. The bond often lingers long after the project wraps up, even if the professional context disappears.

(c) Work Colleagues and Sports Team/Club Members:

Workplaces and sports teams or club settings are another great example of routine-based friendships. You see these people almost every day, share lunch breaks, attend meetings together, or train side by side for hours. This frequent interaction creates a rhythm of connection. Over time, you begin to pick up on their quirks, their habits, and maybe even their pet peeves. You get to know how they respond to stress, what kind of sense of humor they have, and what makes them tick.

In work environments, these friendships can often begin as simple professional exchanges—meeting over deadlines or collaborating on projects. But as you spend more time together, those interactions often move beyond the strictly professional. Maybe you grab coffee together during lunch breaks, swap stories about your weekends, or laugh about the boss's quirky habits. These small, seemingly insignificant moments create bonds that help make the daily grind a little more enjoyable.

In sports teams or clubs, the connection is built through shared passion and effort. Whether you're on a soccer team, training for a marathon, or part of a book club, the routine of meeting up, practicing, or discussing common interests creates a sense of unity. You see each other at your most dedicated and sometimes at your most vulnerable, and that shared commitment often leads to friendship. These friendships can vary in depth. Some might stay strictly in the context of the workplace or the club, while others might spill over into your personal life, and you find yourself hanging out outside of the usual setting.

What's interesting is that these friendships may not always extend beyond the shared space. You might not become close with everyone you work with or train with, but the friendships that do form are often deeply meaningful because they are rooted in daily interaction and shared experiences. These are the people who help you get through the long days, make the mundane more tolerable, and celebrate the little victories with you. Even if you don't hang out outside of work or practice, they are a part of your routine, and that's enough to create a meaningful connection.

3. INTEREST-BASED:

These friendships are formed through shared passions, hobbies, or activities—things you both love to do or enjoy together. The connection between people in these kinds of friendships isn't rooted in convenience, proximity, or sheer repetition; it's based on a genuine love for a particular activity, interest, or experience. When you bond with someone over something you both care deeply about, that connection tends to be deeper and more meaningful because it comes from a place of mutual excitement and passion. These friendships, though often starting around a shared hobby or interest, can evolve into something more personal over time. Here's how these connections typically unfold:

(a) Online Community Friends:

In the modern world, friendships can be formed across continents, and often these relationships grow strong even without face-to-face interaction. The rise of the internet and social media platforms has opened the doors to countless opportunities to meet people who share your interests. Maybe you connect with someone on an online gaming platform, or perhaps you stumble across a photography forum where members share tips and tricks. You might join a Facebook group dedicated to your favorite TV show or a subreddit discussing your hobby or passion.

While these friendships start out as virtual connections, they are often just as real and meaningful as any in-person friendship. These connections are based on shared experiences, discussions, and support, rather than geographic location or shared day-to-day life. The cool part is that, in many cases, you might never meet these people in person. The bond grows through shared interest and mutual understanding, often giving you a sense of belonging and camaraderie. Even if you don't ever have the opportunity to grab a coffee or meet in person, the conversations, the shared excitement over common passions, and the support offered within the community can create a real, lasting friendship. These online communities can become a place where you can be yourself without fear of judgment because everyone is there for the same reasons—whether it's to play a game, discuss a topic, or share knowledge.

For example, you might form a bond with someone who shares your love for a particular genre of music. You both chat about your favorite bands, exchange playlists, and discuss concerts or events. Over time, this virtual friendship might become something more than just sharing music—perhaps you start talking about other aspects of your lives, offer advice during tough times, or celebrate milestones together. These friendships can even evolve into deep, meaningful connections that exist entirely online, transcending the barriers of physical distance.

(b) Hobby Friends:

These are the kinds of friends you meet through shared activities, from art classes to cooking workshops to hiking groups. You start by engaging in an activity you both enjoy, and over time, that common interest forms the base for a friendship. The connection is born out of a shared passion for something you love, but as you spend time together, you begin to discover other things you have in common—whether it's a similar sense of humor, shared life goals, or even a mutual love for good coffee.

For instance, if you've joined a painting class or a pottery workshop, you might start chatting with someone about the different techniques you're learning, discussing your favorite artists, or trading tips on how to improve. After a few classes, you might end up meeting for a coffee to talk more about your craft, or perhaps you find that you both enjoy hiking and decide to plan a weekend trip to explore a new trail together. These hobbies often provide the backdrop for an easy connection, but the friendship itself is built through the shared moments you spend together, the laughs you share, and the memories you create.

These friendships are also incredibly supportive because you're constantly learning and growing together. Whether you're in a group exercise class, a dance class, or a writing group, the camaraderie you build is not just based on the activity but on the way you encourage each other to improve and develop. You may start planning other activities outside of the original hobby, like weekend excursions, dinner parties, or even going to exhibitions or performances related to your shared interest. The joy of these friendships is that they're not just limited to the activity itself—they often grow into full-fledged personal connections.

Moreover, because the foundation of these friendships is based on a shared interest, it's easy to come together again after time apart. Even if you don't see your hobby friends for a while, you can always reconnect over the shared activity that originally brought you together. Whether you're swapping recipes with your cooking class buddies or heading out on a weekend adventure with your hiking group, these friendships are a constant reminder that the best relationships often spring from something as simple as a shared passion.

(c) Event-Based Friends:

Event-based friendships happen in spaces where people gather to learn, network, or experience something new. These could be professional events, workshops, conferences, or even informal gatherings like local meetups or community events. What's interesting about these friendships is that they often start as temporary connections, formed in the context of a single event, but can evolve into long-lasting friendships depending on the interactions during that time.

For example, at a business conference, you might meet someone who's working in a similar field or shares your career aspirations. Over coffee breaks or during workshops, you find that you not only have similar career goals, but also similar interests outside of work, like a love for travel, photography, or a mutual appreciation for certain books. You exchange contact information, and as time passes, you might find yourselves meeting up for coffee regularly to discuss both work-related matters and personal interests.

These event-based friendships can sometimes be fleeting. You might only meet someone once, at a specific event, and not see them again. But in some cases, they turn into more lasting connections. For instance, a networking event might introduce you to a person who becomes a mentor or someone you later collaborate with professionally. In the same way, an academic conference might allow you to meet someone whose research interests align with yours, leading to further conversations and potentially even collaboration on projects.

The beauty of event-based friendships lies in their diversity. Because these relationships are often built around shared goals, interests, or circumstances, they tend to attract people with similar mindsets. They also provide a great way to meet new people outside your immediate circle, expanding your network and introducing you to new perspectives. Whether it's through a professional event or a casual local meetup, these connections often form quickly but can leave a lasting impact on your personal and professional life.

So these are some ways how people come closer, become acquainted, and then you decide to be friends with them or not.

LIFE EXPERIENCE

Reflecting on my journey from childhood to adulthood, I've had the privilege of forging various friendships that have profoundly shaped my life. Though my primary school years were spent in Arunachal Pradesh, those memories feel distant now, as I've lost contact with everyone from that time. Consequently, this narrative begins with my middle school years and extends to the present day.

School Friends

In middle school, our understanding of life was simplistic and largely shaped by our households. At that time, we didn't have the internet or mobile phones to expand our perspectives. Friendships formed naturally, often based on proximity and shared activities. I made several friends whom I called my best friends back then. However, as we grew older, our interests began to diverge, causing some natural distance between us. Over time, new friendships replaced the old ones, creating a pattern of ebb and flow in my social circles.

Even now, a few school friends remain in contact. We occasionally meet during festivals or holidays when we return home from our respective workplaces. Since most of our schoolmates lived in nearby areas, these gatherings feel nostalgic, bringing back fond memories of simpler times. The essence of these friendships lies in their foundation—shared innocence and the unspoken bond of growing up together.

College Friends

College was a transformative period in my life. I attended a government college in Assam, where students from across the state came to study. While not everyone became friends, the hostel experience was a different story altogether. Living in a hostel meant sharing every aspect of life—classes, meals, games, studies, travel, and even the occasional disagreements.

These experiences created a deep camaraderie. We spent 24 hours a day together, forming bonds that often felt like family. Hostel life was a microcosm of society, where we learned to coexist and support one another. These friendships have stood the test of time, and our hostel WhatsApp group remains active to this day. We frequently meet several times a year, cherishing our shared adventures and memories. Whether it's travelling, enjoying a drink, or simply catching up, these friends continue to be an integral part of my life.

University Friends

Pursuing a Master's in Engineering was a unique phase, marked by both academic rigor and personal growth. Most students who enrol in such programmes are either highly meticulous or using the opportunity to prepare for something else while satisfying societal expectations. The two-year course was divided into distinct phases: the first year was intense, with numerous new subjects, exams, and seminars, while the second year offered more freedom as we focused on a year-long project.

We spent countless hours in the laboratory, often working on anything but our projects. This was also the time when we began to enjoy frequent parties and gatherings after college. Our small group was close-knit, without any cliques or divisions. However, as we graduated and embarked on our respective career paths, our interactions gradually diminished. Today, our connections are mostly limited to WhatsApp messages and wedding invitations. These occasions serve as mini-reunions, providing a brief but heartwarming glimpse into the lives of old friends.

Trekking Friends

Living in Pune has introduced me to a new circle of friends—my trekking companions. The Sahyadri range, with its stunning landscapes and challenging trails, has been a significant influence on my lifestyle. I developed a passion for trekking and morning runs, often venturing out alone. This openness to solo adventures has allowed me to meet like-minded individuals who share a love for the outdoors.

Over time, a few of these acquaintances have become regular trekking partners. While we don't usually meet outside of these adventures, we stay connected by inviting each other to upcoming treks. These friendships are uncomplicated and revolve around a shared passion for nature and exploration. Each trek strengthens our bond as we tackle challenges together and marvel at the beauty of the Sahyadris.

From middle school to my current adventures, each phase of life has gifted me a distinct set of friendships, each shaping me in its own way. School friends instilled the values of innocence and unwavering loyalty, while college companions opened my eyes to the joys of sharing life's highs and lows in close quarters. University friends emphasised the delicate balance between hard work and moments of leisure, and trekking companions now fuel my spirit with their zest for exploration and adventure.

Though vastly different, these friendships are bound by a common thread—they've profoundly influenced my growth and enriched my journey in ways words can barely capture. Whether it's sharing laughter over nostalgic memories, marking life's milestones together, or stepping into uncharted territories, these bonds highlight the beauty of human connection. Over the years, I've learned that while friendships evolve with time and circumstance, their core—the shared experiences and genuine understanding—remains a cherished and unchanging part of life.

WHY SOME FRIENDSHIP LASTS?

Friendship, I've realized, is a complex and multifaceted thing. It doesn't always follow a set of rules or expectations. For instance, there are a few friends in my life who don't ever bother sending a WhatsApp message, and you can forget about a phone call from them! Yet, despite this, when we do cross paths—whether it's at a random get-together, a wedding, or even a chance meeting on the street—it feels like nothing has changed. We slip right back into that easy rhythm, laughing, chatting, and reminiscing as if no time has passed at all. It's almost like we have our own unspoken understanding, where the strength of our bond doesn't rely on constant communication or grand gestures, but rather on the shared moments we've built together in the past. That's when it hit me: true friendship isn't necessarily about the frequency of interaction, but about the quality of the connection that endures regardless of time or distance.

When I thought about it more, I came to realize that there are a few key ingredients that keep these kinds of friendships going strong, even if we don't talk every day. First, there's the shared history—the moments and experiences that create a solid foundation for the relationship. It could be from school, college, work, or just random life encounters. These moments are the glue that holds the friendship together, and even if life takes you in different directions, that foundation remains unshaken. Second, there's a mutual understanding of space. It's the unspoken rule that no one has to constantly check in, yet when you meet, it feels as if you've been talking all along. Finally, there's the acceptance of one another as we are, without judgment or expectation. It's not about keeping up with every little detail of each other's life but accepting that life moves on and, despite the gaps, the friendship remains untouched. When all these elements come together, it's as though time stands still whenever we reconnect, and that's the magic of it.

1. Emotional Connection

Friendship, when you really think about it, is often built on shared values and interests. The connection usually starts with something in common, whether it's a mutual passion, similar views on life, or just being drawn to the same things. This could be anything, from cheering for the same football team to having similar takes on the latest trends, debates, or pop culture. That common ground acts as a bridge, making initial interactions feel smoother and more natural. It's like meeting someone who already speaks the same language as you, and suddenly, you feel understood. This is what makes the process of getting to know each other feel so easy and enjoyable. It creates a sense of camaraderie, where you're not just two random people, but teammates navigating life together. When those shared interests and values align, it creates an unspoken bond that strengthens over time, making the relationship feel not just like a friendship, but more like a partnership.

The next crucial ingredient in lasting friendships is mutual support. True friends are those who show up when it really matters. They might not always be there for every little moment, but when life throws a curveball, they're the ones who have your back. It's not about constant presence, but knowing that when things get tough, you have someone who will listen, offer comfort, or simply be there for you in silence. Think about the friend who's ready to listen to your venting after a stressful day at work, or the one who knows exactly how to lift your spirits when you're feeling down. These seemingly small acts of support build over time, creating a rock-solid foundation that keeps friendships intact, even when life gets complicated. It's comforting to have that assurance, knowing that, no matter what life throws your way, there's a friend who will stand by you, even if it's just to say, "I get it, life sucks sometimes."

And of course, there's emotional investment—the lifeblood of any relationship. Friendships, like plants, need a little care to grow and thrive. It's about the small things—the check-in messages, remembering someone's birthday, or making time for a quick coffee catch-up—that keep the connection fresh and vibrant. These little acts are like deposits into a friendship bank, and over time, they accumulate, strengthening the bond between two people. Some friendships are low-maintenance, thriving with minimal interaction, while others need constant attention to flourish. Regardless of the style, the investment of time, energy, and emotional presence is what sustains a friendship, keeping it alive and kicking for the long haul. In the end, it's not the grand gestures, but the consistent, small acts of care that make the bond stronger, allowing the friendship to endure, even when life gets busy or complicated. These are the foundations of a friendship that can weather any storm.

PERSONAL EXPERIENCE:

Reflecting on my journey from childhood to adulthood, friendships have played a pivotal role in shaping my emotional landscape. During our school days, we were naive and didn't give much thought to whom we befriended. Even when our parents advised us against associating with certain kids, we rarely heeded their warnings. Perhaps it was because we shared an unspoken connection—whether through mischief, play, or common interests.

However, as the years passed, many of those friendships became sporadic. Life's busy schedules and diverging paths meant that we inevitably drifted apart. Still, the memories of those carefree days remain precious.

Engineering college, on the other hand, was a transformative phase in my life. The friendships I formed during this time have been some of the most enduring. Among them, the hostel boys hold a particularly special place in my heart. Living together for four years forged an unbreakable bond. We didn't just share rooms; we shared countless experiences—from late-night study sessions and heartfelt conversations to impromptu adventures. These moments created a camaraderie that has stood the test of time. Even now, most of us remain close, often planning trips or meeting up for a drink whenever we can. The joy and support we continue to derive from these friendships are a testament to their strength.

Emotional connection is an essential aspect of any friendship, yet it's not something that can be forced—it happens naturally. As the saying goes, "You're the average of the five people you spend the most time with." In many ways, we are drawn to those who share a similar mindset and outlook on life. This alignment forms the foundation for meaningful relationships that endure through life's ups and downs.

Whether it's the innocence of childhood friendships, the intensity of hostel life, or the fleeting connections made during higher studies, each relationship has played a vital role in my personal growth. These friendships, rooted in shared experiences and emotional understanding, continue to shape who I am today.

2. Communication and Conflict Resolution

Effective communication forms the bedrock of strong friendships. It's not just about talking endlessly or sharing every little detail of your day. It's about the deeper, more meaningful exchanges that happen when two people feel completely comfortable and safe with each other. Great friendships allow for a kind of openness where both people feel they can truly express themselves—without fear of judgment or ridicule. This doesn't always have to be serious or heavy; it could be as simple as telling your friend about your day or discussing a hilarious thing that happened at work. But it's the honesty in these interactions that matter. The best friendships are those where you're not only heard but also understood. It's a space where you can be yourself—no pretensions, no facades. Whether it's talking about your biggest dreams or your worst fears, the communication flows freely, and both friends feel valued and appreciated. Even when life is chaotic or you're in a rush, a good friendship lets you pick up right where you left off, as if no time has passed. It's these kinds of exchanges that foster trust and create a bond that feels both effortless and powerful.

Then comes healthy conflict resolution, which is just as crucial. Let's face it, no friendship is free from disagreements or misunderstandings. Whether it's a trivial matter, like arguing about the best pizza place, or something more significant, like one person feeling neglected, the ability to handle conflict without letting it ruin the friendship is key. In any long-lasting relationship, differences will arise, and how you address them can make or break the connection. The best friends know that it's not about avoiding conflict altogether—it's about navigating it with respect and understanding. Rather than letting the issue linger, good friends confront the problem head-on, having an open and honest conversation about what went wrong. It's about clearing the air and expressing feelings without letting things fester into resentment. For example, if one friend tends to be late for meetups or cancels plans last minute, instead of letting irritation build, they'll calmly talk it out, offering understanding and coming up with solutions. This doesn't always mean there are no hard feelings, but it does mean that the friendship matters more than the issue at hand. Over time, these little resolutions help create a deeper bond, as both friends learn to navigate conflict with maturity and empathy. What truly makes a friendship resilient is the ability to disagree without disrespecting each other and to move past challenges without holding grudges. In the end, it's not the absence of conflict but the way conflicts are handled that strengthens the friendship and makes it enduring. This openness to handle issues with care and clarity ensures that the relationship doesn't just survive but thrives, even when things get tough.

PERSONAL EXPERIENCE:

Tantrums, petty fights, and reconciliation are all part of human relationships. The fact that we can still maintain friendships despite these moments speaks volumes about the strength of our bonds.I must admit, holding onto grudges has always been a bit of an issue for me. I'm not someone who throws tantrums or gets into fights unnecessarily, but when it does happen, I tend to carry the feelings for far too long. I'm aware this isn't the healthiest trait, and I do try to improve, but that's just how I've been for as long as I can remember.School days were different. We were kids, and fights back then were often silly and short-lived. As we grew older, many of those arguments faded from memory as we matured. Things changed during college, though. In those teenage years, with emotions running high and egos clashing, fights became more frequent and often more intense.I still vividly remember an argument I had during my third semester. It was with my roommate, and the fight happened during a fresher's introduction session in our juniors' class. The disagreement was brief but intense, and for a while, we avoided speaking to each other, even outside of class. However, since we shared a room, it was impossible to avoid each other entirely. Over time, we moved past the formalities, and things gradually returned to normal. What helped was the mutual understanding we developed—we both remembered what had triggered the fight and made a conscious effort not to cross those lines again.During my Master's programme, I experienced a verbal clash with a girl over an attendance issue. This one lingered far longer than most. The fight started with heated words in person and spilled over into our WhatsApp group. The tension lasted for three days of arguments, followed by months of ignoring each other. It wasn't until a New Year's picnic by the Brahmaputra River, where all our batchmates gathered, that we began to mend things. Even then, the connection wasn't the same. The fight left a mark, and while the bitterness faded over time, a certain distance remained.Years later, the remnants of that grudge have all but disappeared. I even attended her wedding, genuinely happy for her. It's funny how time and perspective can soften even the sharpest memories.These experiences taught me that while conflict is inevitable, how we handle it determines the outcome of our relationships. Holding onto anger only weighs you down. Though I still have room for growth, I'm learning to let go more quickly and focus on preserving meaningful connections. At the end of the day, the people who matter are worth the effort of reconciliation, no matter how challenging it may feel in the moment.

3. Adaptability and Context

Adaptability to change is perhaps one of the most important qualities that separates a passing acquaintance from a lifelong friend. Life is anything but static—people grow, evolve, and face new challenges. Jobs change, cities get swapped for new ones, relationships form, and families are built. In all of this, a true friend is someone who understands that life's transitions might pull you in different directions, but they are willing to adjust without the friendship unraveling. Take, for example, the weekends you used to spend together with your closest friend. Over time, your schedules shift. Maybe you get a new job with long hours or move to a different part of town. Initially, it feels strange not having that regular catch-up, but instead of drifting apart, a true friend finds ways to keep the connection going. You might go from seeing each other every week to once a month, but the bond remains strong. It's not the frequency of interaction that matters but the effort you put into making time for each other. What's truly remarkable about such friendships is that they bend and adapt to the new circumstances. The change in frequency or form of your connection doesn't signify the end of a friendship—it just requires both people to be flexible and willing to make adjustments. A friendship that can weather change, even if it's just a matter of finding a new rhythm, is a friendship that will last. The key is maintaining the understanding that your connection doesn't rely on what it used to be, but rather on the effort both of you are still willing to put in to sustain it, despite the changes that life inevitably brings.

External factors also play a huge role in shaping the course of friendships. Sometimes, these factors are beyond our control, and they can influence the dynamics of a relationship in profound ways. Social circles shift, responsibilities grow, and life stages change. For example, friendships formed in school or university often face the test of time once everyone moves on to different places, whether for further studies or a job. People naturally get busy, and priorities shift. The friend who was once just a phone call away may suddenly become someone you see only on holidays, or sometimes not at all. However, external circumstances don't have to mean the end of a friendship. If the foundation of the relationship is strong, you'll both find ways to stay connected. For example, even though you may live far apart, you could create new ways to stay in touch—like video calls or even sending postcards from your travels. Some friends might even create small traditions that keep the bond alive, like planning an annual get-together or even just sending each other a text once a week to check in. It's these little acts of effort that help maintain the connection over time and distance. Interestingly, sometimes the bond becomes even stronger because of the effort it takes to stay in each other's lives. It's almost as though the distance and the challenges make you realize just how important that friendship truly is. As the saying goes, "The best friendships are those that withstand the test of time and distance." In the end, it's the mutual effort to adjust to life's unpredictable twists that strengthens a friendship and helps it grow, even as the world around you changes. This adaptability, both in terms of frequency and approach, ensures that friendships not only survive but thrive in the face of life's many transitions.

In the end, I've come to realize that friendships aren't some rigid checklist you have to follow in order to be deemed "successful." Rather, they're about finding a balance that feels right to you. They're like different threads woven into the fabric of your life—each thread adding its own color and texture. Some friends are the kind you see every day, the ones who are around for the mundane, day-to-day moments. You share coffee breaks, catch up on the latest gossip, and are there for each other through thick and thin. Then there are the friends who, though not around every day, manage to pop up just when you need them the most. These friendships may not be constant, but when they show up, it's like no time has passed at all. You pick up right where you left off, and suddenly, it feels like the connection you share is even more profound because it has been able to endure time apart.

And then there are those friends who surprise you—the ones who you might only see once a year, yet when you do, it's like everything falls into place. These are the friends who, despite the infrequent encounters, leave a lasting impact on your life. It's the ones who, in rare moments of deep conversation or shared laughter, remind you of who you are at your core. It's like these friends carry a certain magic, an ability to make you feel deeply connected even without constant interaction. You may not be texting every day or planning frequent meet-ups, but there's something about those interactions that resonate deeply, as though they transcend the physical distance. These friendships, though far and few between, often have the ability to be incredibly impactful, even in short bursts. They show you that distance and time don't always dictate the strength of a bond. In fact, some of the most meaningful connections in life are the ones that happen unexpectedly or sporadically.

It's like a recipe for life. You need a little bit of everything to create the perfect mix. Each friend, whether they're a daily presence or a rare encounter, adds their own unique flavor to your world. Some friends are there through every high and low, offering unwavering support and consistency. Others bring an occasional spark of excitement or nostalgia, lifting your spirits with just a few moments of time together. Together, these friendships create a vibrant tapestry, rich with diverse experiences, and the beauty of it all is that they don't need to be perfectly balanced all the time. Sometimes, one type of friendship might take precedence for a while, but as life ebbs and flows, so do the friendships that surround you.

So, here's to all the friends in our lives—the ones who are nearby, the ones who are scattered across the world, and the ones who come out of nowhere and remind us just how much we matter to each other. Some friendships might require more effort to maintain, others thrive effortlessly, but all of them, no matter their form, contribute something valuable to our lives. Cheers to those who brighten our days with their presence, even if it's just a text away, and to those who make an appearance at special occasions like weddings, reminding us that some of the most meaningful friendships are the ones that endure despite the passage of time. Each friend, whether you talk to them every day or only once a year, has a unique role to play in your life story. And for that, we should be grateful.

PERSONAL EXPERIENCE:

There are some friends we don't speak to often or see regularly, yet they remain in our contact lists or WhatsApp groups. But when we do get the chance to meet, it's like no time has passed—we thoroughly enjoy each other's company and share some quality moments together.

One such reunion happened during a visit to Gurgaon, where I reconnected with my school friend, Jayshankar, after 11 long years. I was in Delhi as part of my trip to Bir Billing for my first paragliding adventure. While planning my journey, I discovered that Jayshankar lived in Gurgaon and worked in Delhi's Connaught Place.

I reached out to him, not only to catch up but also to ask for a small favour—whether I could leave some extra luggage at his place, as I didn't want to lug around heavy bags while travelling. Thankfully, he agreed, and that set the stage for our much-anticipated catch-up.

When we finally met, it was like stepping back in time. We reminisced about our school days, sharing laughter over silly stories and fond memories. It felt so natural, as though those 11 years had simply melted away.

Reunions like this remind me of the enduring nature of some friendships. Even when life takes us in different directions and we go years without seeing each other, the bond remains strong. Spending time with Janta that day brought back a flood of nostalgia and a renewed sense of gratitude for those lasting connections.

It was more than just catching up—it was a celebration of old times and a reminder of how friendships, even the ones we don't nurture every day, can continue to bring joy and warmth to our lives when we least expect it.

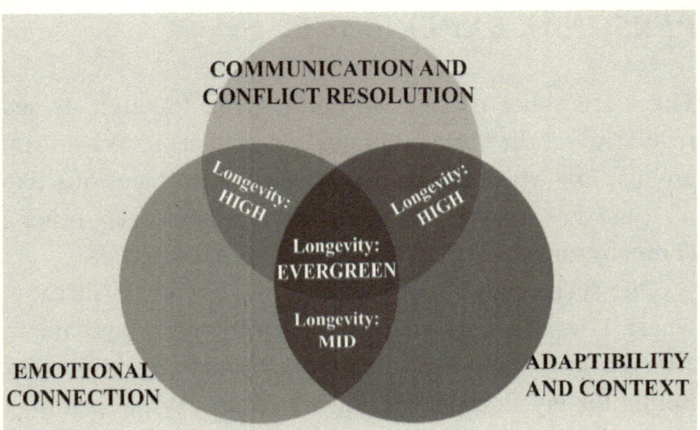

Friendship Longevity Venn Diagram

Explaining Overlapping Areas

1. Emotional Connection + Communication & Conflict Resolution:

Friendships that are built on both emotional connection and effective communication are often the strongest and most enduring. These friendships thrive on a deep sense of trust, where both individuals feel comfortable being vulnerable with each other. They are not just about having fun or passing the time; they are rooted in genuine care and understanding. This emotional bond fosters loyalty, and both friends are there for each other, no matter what.

What truly sets these friendships apart is their ability to weather conflict. Disagreements or misunderstandings don't tear them apart because there's a foundation of open communication. When challenges arise, these friends talk things through, listen to each other's perspectives, and work together to find solutions. This ability to resolve conflicts, combined with emotional support, strengthens their bond even further.

Because these friendships are built on such solid ground, they have the potential to last through various phases of life. Whether it's moving to a new city, changing jobs, or facing personal struggles, they can endure these shifts. Life circumstances may change, but the mutual understanding, trust, and support that these friendships are built on don't easily fade.

Longevity: High. These friendships are likely to last a lifetime because of the emotional depth and consistent, open communication that keeps them strong and resilient.

2. Communication & Conflict Resolution + Adaptability & Context:

Friendships that are adaptable and communicative are built on the ability to handle life's ups and downs while navigating through conflict in a healthy way. These friendships rely on open communication and a willingness to adjust to each other's evolving circumstances. For example, friends who can discuss their differences calmly and without resentment are able to work through challenges together, keeping the relationship intact. They can also adjust to changes in life, such as moving to a new city, changing careers, or entering new relationships, without losing touch.

However, while these friendships are functional and can weather a lot, they may not always feel as deeply connected. Without a strong emotional bond, the connection may be more about convenience or habit than true intimacy. Over time, these friendships may feel less fulfilling, even if they remain steady. Emotional depth is what makes a friendship truly special—without it, the friendship can sometimes feel more like an arrangement or routine than a meaningful relationship.

Longevity: Medium; These types of friendships tend to have a medium to high chance of lasting over time, as long as both people continue to invest in maintaining the relationship. But, if the emotional connection is shallow, they may gradually lose their significance. Though they can endure through various life changes, the lack of deeper connection might lead to a sense of emotional distance in the long run.

3. Adaptability & Context + Emotional Connection:

Friendships that are built on a strong emotional connection and adaptability are deeply rooted, making them resilient in the face of life's inevitable changes. These friendships thrive because, even when life circumstances shift—whether due to moving to a new city, changing jobs, or facing personal challenges—there is a deep emotional bond that holds them together. The connection remains steady, even when time or distance comes between the friends.

Although these friendships may not always excel in resolving conflicts, the emotional strength between the individuals often fills that gap. When disagreements or misunderstandings arise, these friends may not always have the perfect solution right away, but their underlying trust and understanding allow them to navigate through those moments. Sometimes, they may even avoid confrontation to protect the relationship, which is a common dynamic in emotionally close friendships.

What makes these friendships enduring is their ability to adapt to life's changes. They are flexible, and both people in the relationship understand that sometimes life gets in the way of constant communication or perfect harmony. But despite these occasional hurdles, the emotional bond remains intact, and that is what keeps the friendship strong.

Longevity: High; these friendships often last for many years because they can weather change, adapt, and still maintain a sense of closeness and mutual care, even when things aren't perfect.

4. Centre (All Three Overlap)- The Most Enduring Friendships:

Friendships that combine emotional connection, strong communication, conflict resolution skills, and adaptability are the most resilient and enduring. These friendships are built on a solid emotional bond where both individuals genuinely care for each other and share a sense of trust. What sets them apart is the ability to communicate openly and honestly, addressing issues as they arise rather than letting them fester. This enables them to resolve conflicts constructively and come out stronger on the other side.

Moreover, these friendships are adaptable, adjusting to the natural changes life brings. Whether it's a new job, a change in location, or shifts in personal circumstances, these friends are able to find new ways to stay connected and supportive. They don't crumble under pressure or distance but find ways to evolve, making them incredibly resilient.

Longevity: Very High. They stand the test of time because they are rooted in mutual understanding, emotional support, and the ability to weather life's ups and downs. They don't just survive—they thrive, becoming even more meaningful with time. These friendships are the ones that can last a lifetime, constantly evolving but always remaining grounded in the trust and connection that first brought them together. They are the true pillars of emotional support and personal growth throughout the years.

CHAPTER THREE

UNDERSTANDING TOXICITY

The American Psychological Association (APA) and research on toxic relationships have shown that negative friendships can indeed have a significant impact on mental health. Toxic friendships, where one person consistently belittles, criticizes, or manipulates the other, can contribute to heightened levels of stress, anxiety, and lower self-esteem. According to a study published in the Journal of Social and Personal Relationships, individuals with toxic friends reported higher stress and decreased life satisfaction compared to those with supportive social networks. This is because toxic friendships can create a constant emotional burden, leading people to feel insecure, inadequate, or even guilty without cause. Dr. Ramani Durvasula, a clinical psychologist, also highlights the detrimental effects of toxic friendships, explaining that such relationships can undermine self-worth. Regular criticism and belittling behavior from friends can make individuals question their own value and feel responsible for issues within the friendship. Such effects can lead to a cycle of self-doubt and emotional strain, which may require therapeutic intervention for recovery.

When it comes to managing friendships that aren't as healthy as we'd like them to be, setting boundaries is often the first step in preserving your peace of mind. Sometimes, reducing contact or, if necessary, completely ending the relationship can be incredibly liberating. Of course, not all toxic friendships can be easily severed, especially if there are shared social circles, work dynamics, or family ties involved. In those situations, managing how you interact with that person becomes crucial. It might mean keeping the conversations brief or limiting emotional engagement. Practicing self-affirmation strategies—reminding yourself of your worth and reinforcing your boundaries—can make a huge difference in lessening the psychological impact of these relationships.

Now, I'm not here to offer any professional psychological advice, but I do believe in the importance of reflecting on the friendships in your life and how they affect your well-being. Friendships, at their core, should bring joy, support, and mutual growth. If they start to feel more draining than fulfilling, it's time to evaluate what role they truly play in your life. Friendships should add to your happiness and help you grow into the best version of yourself. If they're taking more than they're giving, it's essential to be honest with yourself and consider whether they're worth continuing.

Over time, I've developed a little framework or categorization for friendships, which has helped me navigate through the inevitable bumps and challenges that come up. It's not about cutting people off arbitrarily but understanding what type of friendships nourish you and which ones might need a little more space or boundaries. Here's my take on it:

S. No	LEVEL	CHARACTERISTICS	EXAMPLES	IMPACT
1	MINOR ANNOYANCES	• Small annoyances or habits that is easy to overlook. • Typical in close friendships due to personality quirks.	• Different taste in food and drinks. • Friends pushing Messy habits.	MINOR IRRITATIONS, TOLERABLE
2	SMALL TANTRUMS	• Recurring conflicts or lifestyle clashes. • Often disrupts routines and requires communication.	• Roommates skipping shared chores. • Pressure to drink or party.	FRUSTRATING, MANAGEABLE
3	BOUNDARIES VIOLATED	• Serious overstepping of personal boundaries. • Causes distress, discomfort or moral conflict.	• Disrespect for personal values and limits. • Invasion of Privacy.	HIGH STRESS, POTENTIAL TOXICITY

Levels of Toxicity in friendships

MINOR ANNOYANCES

The Unlikeable But Tolerable Stuff

Friendships are often the spaces where we experience some of the most relatable, and sometimes, the most amusing quirks. These are the minor annoyances that we all deal with in one way or another. And let's be honest—if you haven't had a few eye-roll moments or had to bite your tongue when hanging out with your friends, then maybe you're in a movie, or you've yet to spend enough time with someone to really get to know their true colors. In the real world, friendships come with those quirks—little differences in habits, tastes, or preferences that tend to be harmless but occasionally make you stop and think, "Well, that's just them." These kinds of annoyances don't create deep problems or serious conflicts but are part of the charm of truly getting to know someone. In fact, they often make the bond deeper and more authentic. Below are a few examples of these everyday, “small stuff” annoyances that, while slightly frustrating, actually add to the uniqueness of any friendship.

(a) Food Preferences

This one is a classic. Imagine being a die-hard Sprite fan. It’s your go-to drink, the one that, no matter what, always tastes just right. But there’s always that friend who insists on grabbing Coca-Cola instead. You’ve heard their arguments: "Coke is just better," or "It’s the classic!" Sure, you roll your eyes, wishing they’d see the light and join you on team Sprite. But do you fight over it? No. You take a sip of their Coke and make a joke about it, knowing deep down it’s not a battle worth fighting. The reality is, it’s just a drink, and your friendship is way bigger than that small difference. And honestly, if this is the biggest annoyance you face in a friendship, you’re probably in a pretty solid one. The world won’t stop spinning because of a soda preference, but it does add a layer of light-heartedness to your interactions.

(b) Lack of Neatness

Let’s be real—who doesn’t like a tidy, organized space? You’re the type who keeps your socks neatly in the drawer, your desk organized, and your living space just the right amount of cozy. You know where everything is, and if something’s out of place, it bugs you just a little. But then, there’s your friend—the one who seems to think the living room is a personal storage space. Socks scattered on the floor, dirty dishes piling up in the sink, books or clothes left in random places. At first, it drives you a bit crazy. You find yourself tidying up the space when no one's looking or silently sighing at the pile of laundry. And yet, somehow, you accept it. It's a part of who they are, and, in the grand scheme of things, it doesn't matter. You've learned to adjust, to work around the clutter, and even to appreciate the casualness they bring to the situation. Their messiness doesn't diminish your connection; it just adds a little humor to the mix. The truth is, this kind of difference is usually one of the less dramatic annoyances in any friendship. The fact that your friend feels comfortable enough to be themselves in your space speaks volumes. And honestly, it doesn't take much to throw a blanket over the mess or grab a few extra snacks for the night.

(c) Health Choices

We've all been there. You're trying to eat clean, you're meal prepping for the week, and you've even cut back on processed foods in favor of salads and whole grains. It feels good—your body's thanking you for making healthier choices. But there's always that group of friends who are firmly in the "junk-food is life" camp. They order pizza, burgers, fries, and whatever deep-fried goodness they can get their hands on. And while you're over here with your salad, trying to stick to your new routine, they're looking at you like you've committed a crime against taste buds. Sometimes they'll even tease you, calling you a "party pooper" for refusing to dive into the pizza pile with them. Do you give in to the temptation? Well, maybe once or twice. But you know, deep down, you're staying strong for your health. But you don't make a big deal about it.

You smile, laugh it off, and go back to your salad, secretly wishing they'd switch their fries for something healthier. You've learned that it's okay to be the odd one out when it comes to food choices, and these little compromises only add to the bond you share. And let's face it, it's not always about being "right" or "healthy"—it's about the good times spent together.

These minor annoyances may seem trivial, but they are an essential part of any real friendship. They create the kind of relationships that are based on acceptance and understanding. You get to know your friends in ways that no one else does—sometimes through their weird food preferences, their cluttered living rooms, or their unashamed indulgence in junk food. While these differences may make you want to roll your eyes or have a private laugh, you wouldn't trade them for the world. They add character to the friendship, making the bond deeper and more human. Without them, everything might feel too perfect, too easy, and, let's face it, a little boring. These quirks are the seasoning that makes the whole friendship flavorful and interesting. Without them, the connection would lack that spark that makes it truly special. So next time your friend orders Coke when you've clearly stated you're a Sprite person, or leaves their shoes all over your place, just smile and remember—these little annoyances are what make the friendship real.

LIFE EXPERIENCE:

When I first moved into my hostel, I shared a room with two other boys. At first, it was a great setup. We got along well, shared a few laughs, and made the room feel like a little haven amidst the chaos of hostel life. However, things took a turn when one of my roommates became too friendly. While his sociable nature was admirable, it led to our room becoming a hub for endless visitors.

Friends and acquaintances would pop in at all hours, turning our small space into a public discussion area. What started as a minor annoyance quickly escalated into a persistent problem. I found myself unable to concentrate or relax, as the constant stream of people disrupted our peace. Eventually, I decided enough was enough and requested to change my room. While this decision wasn't easy, it was the right one. Fortunately, my relationship with my friendly roommate didn't suffer—we simply acknowledged that living together wasn't the best fit for us.

FRUSTRATIONS

Small Tantrums/Disagreements

Friendships are one of the greatest joys in life, but they can also be a source of frustration. As wonderful as they are, every friendship will eventually face some bumps along the way. You know those moments when you feel your patience is being tested, whether it's because of a friend's annoying habit, something they said, or their behavior in a certain situation? These little irritations can often feel like no big deal at first, but if they keep happening, they can slowly chip away at the bond you share. If ignored, they might even become bigger issues, threatening the connection you've built over time. The secret is to address these frustrations early before they turn into something more serious. Here are some classic examples of situations where frustrations tend to build up:

(a) Shared Responsibilities

One of the most common sources of tension between friends arises from shared responsibilities, especially in living situations or group projects. When you live with someone or work together on a shared task, it's expected that duties will be split evenly. But that's not always how it works out. Maybe you find yourself cleaning more often, doing most of the cooking, or handling things like bills or organizing plans. At first, it seems like a small inconvenience, but when it becomes a recurring issue, frustration starts to build. The problem intensifies when the other person seems oblivious or "forgets" to do their part. You begin to feel like you're doing the heavy lifting, and resentment can start to creep in. If left unchecked, this imbalance in shared responsibilities can put a real strain on a friendship. The best way to handle this is through an open conversation. Discussing your expectations and addressing fairness head-on can resolve these frustrations before they cause bigger rifts.

(b) Lifestyle Differences

Another issue that can create tension in friendships is lifestyle differences. It's common for friends to have different routines, preferences, and habits, but when these differences start to affect your interactions, they can become a problem. For example, maybe you're an early riser who loves peace and quiet in the mornings, but your friends are night owls who like to stay up late, making noise or staying engaged in activities. While it's not malicious, it can become extremely frustrating. The lack of sleep affects your mood and energy levels, and suddenly, your once pleasant hangouts are marred by irritability. These kinds of lifestyle differences can cause long-term tension if not managed properly. The solution here lies in finding a compromise that works for everyone. Perhaps you can set quiet hours, or if you know you'll be staying over, agree to be mindful of each other's schedules. Mutual respect for differing lifestyles can help maintain harmony.

(c) Financial Habits

Money is a sensitive topic, but it can also cause significant stress in friendships, especially when your financial habits don't align. You might be trying to save money for a big goal, whether it's a vacation, a car, or just getting your finances in order, while your friends are more spontaneous, spending freely on nights out, dinners, or extravagant trips. Over time, this disparity can lead to frustration. If you constantly have to say "no" to activities because they don't fit within your budget, you may start to feel left out or like you're missing out on the fun. On the other hand, if you agree to go along with their plans, it can strain your finances and cause additional stress. The key here is to be honest and upfront about your financial situation. If you explain your goals and your current limitations, your friends will likely understand and be more considerate. You might even find that they're open to suggesting more budget-friendly hangouts or activities that are equally enjoyable without putting a strain on your finances.

As these little annoyances build up over time, it's easy to start letting them slide or hope that they will resolve themselves. However, when frustration is left unaddressed, it can grow into something much bigger. Ignoring these issues can lead to passive-aggressive behavior, unspoken resentment, or even full-blown arguments. The key to avoiding this escalation is to address your frustrations directly with your friends, but in a calm and constructive manner. The goal is not to attack or blame, but to express how you feel and open up a space for understanding. Approach the situation with the intention of finding a solution together, rather than letting your frustration turn into an argument. Most of the time, these issues are easier to solve than we initially think, and a little open communication can go a long way in smoothing things over.

Friendships require effort, and while it's normal to have differences, it's important to address them when they begin to affect the quality of the relationship. Remember, friendships are about mutual understanding, respect, and compromise. A little patience, a lot of understanding, and a willingness to have those sometimes difficult conversations can help prevent small annoyances from turning into something more destructive. After all, the best friendships are built on the ability to work through challenges together.

LIFE EXPERIENCE:

A similar situation arose during my university years, but on a much larger scale. It wasn't just a matter of difficult roommates—it was the entire hostel environment that became unbearable. The atmosphere was rife with problems: ragging, fights, late-night shouting matches, and general chaos.

For two years, I endured it, hoping things would improve. Eventually, I realised that the stress was affecting my studies and mental well-being. I decided to leave the hostel and move into a private paying guest (PG) accommodation. The change was like a breath of fresh air. I finally had a quieter space to focus on my work and unwind after a long day. It taught me the importance of prioritising my own peace over trying to adapt to a toxic environment.

BOUNDARIES VIOLATED

Beyond Bearable

At some point, every friendship will go through ups and downs. But when things start shifting into unhealthy territory, it's crucial to recognize the warning signs. This is the stage where the casual annoyances that you may have once brushed off begin to transform into something much more serious. No longer is it about harmless quirks or small habits—it's about situations where you feel uncomfortable, disrespected, or even emotionally drained. These kinds of situations are not about differences in taste or opinion; they're about boundaries being crossed. When these boundaries are consistently ignored, it may be time to step back and evaluate whether the relationship is worth maintaining. Here's what that might look like in real life:

(a) Privacy Invasion

Privacy is one of the most fundamental aspects of personal space. You've always been someone who values their own space, who's selective about who they invite into your home, and who likes to keep certain details of your life private. But suddenly, things start to change. Your friends might begin to invite people into your home without asking first, or they may show up at your door unannounced, assuming it's perfectly fine. It's no longer about a small inconvenience; it's about your personal boundaries being disregarded. It's the feeling of being unsettled in your own space—when your home, your personal sanctuary, doesn't feel like your own anymore. This invasion isn't just about unexpected guests, but also about the feeling of being disregarded. When friends start pushing these boundaries, it's a clear sign that they no longer respect your privacy, and that can be emotionally taxing. You may feel like you're constantly on edge, wondering if your space is truly your own.

(b) Peer Pressure

Peer pressure doesn't just happen in high school—it can occur well into adulthood, especially within groups of friends. Imagine being someone who doesn't drink or doesn't want to participate in certain activities, and yet your friends don't respect that choice. Instead, they continually bring alcohol to your house or make plans that they know you don't feel comfortable with. You politely decline, but it doesn't stop there. They press you to join in, joke about it, or even guilt-trip you into feeling bad for not partaking. It's no longer about having fun together; it becomes about making you feel alienated for sticking to your personal choices. The pressure starts to feel overwhelming. What should be a fun, casual hangout turns into a battle of wills. No matter how many times you say no, they keep pushing. At this point, it's not just about harmless fun; it's about your personal boundaries being violated. The worst part? You feel like the odd one out, and you start questioning whether these people truly care about respecting your decisions, or if they just want you to conform to their expectations.

(c) Crossing Moral Boundaries

Moral values are what guide our actions and decisions in life. Everyone has a set of beliefs, some of which might be deeply personal and rooted in ethics or personal experiences. For example, you may have a strong stance against substance use or find certain behaviors unethical. However, your friends start pushing you to participate in activities that go against your values. They might be engaging in risky behaviors or encouraging you to join in, dismissing your discomfort. When this happens, it's not just about an awkward situation—it's about feeling pressured to compromise your beliefs just to fit in. At this point, it's no longer about fun or friendship—it's about respect for your values. When your friends don't respect your moral boundaries, it's a clear sign that they may not have your best interests at heart. This kind of behavior forces you to reconsider if these friendships are truly healthy, or if they are toxic and emotionally draining.

When these behaviors—whether it's invasion of privacy, peer pressure, or the crossing of moral boundaries—begin to surface in your friendships, it's essential to take a step back and assess the relationship. Friendships should be built on mutual respect, understanding, and trust. If these qualities are no longer present, it may be time to have an honest conversation with your friends about how their actions are affecting you. If they fail to acknowledge your concerns or continue disregarding your boundaries, you might have to create some space. In the long run, keeping relationships that push you into uncomfortable situations will only wear you down emotionally. Healthy friendships are those where both people can thrive without the need to compromise who they are. A true friend will respect your boundaries, values, and choices, without making you feel pressured or uncomfortable. If you find yourself consistently doubting your friendship, remember that your well-being should always come first. True friends will understand that and will always support you in maintaining your emotional health.

LIFE EXPERIENCE:

While I haven't personally faced this, my friend Pranjit once shared a troubling experience that highlighted the importance of compatible flatmates. He was living in a shared accommodation provided by his workplace. Being in a good position at his company, he expected a certain level of maturity and respect from his flatmates. Unfortunately, his flatmates—who worked in blue-collar roles such as drivers and technicians—lacked basic civic sense.

To clarify, this isn't a generalisation about people in those roles, but rather an observation about the specific individuals he lived with. These four boys would create a mess, disregard cleanliness, and often invade his personal space. Despite being a tolerant and understanding person, Pranjit found it increasingly difficult to coexist with them. Eventually, he moved out, a decision that restored his peace of mind and reaffirmed his boundaries.

CHAPTER FOUR

FINDING BALANCE

I hope you've taken the time to read and reflect on the previous chapter and understand the concept of setting boundaries in friendships. It's a crucial skill that helps maintain healthy relationships, but, let's be honest, setting boundaries isn't always as simple as it sounds. Sometimes, the lines aren't as clear-cut as we might hope. Boundaries can be complex, nuanced, and easily misunderstood. Often, we find ourselves in situations where we've invested a lot of time and energy into a friendship, only to realize, sometimes far too late, that things have crossed a line. The warning signs can be subtle, and before you know it, you've unknowingly pushed a boundary or ignored one yourself. This can lead to misunderstandings or, worse, the breakdown of a once-strong relationship.

It's easy to get caught up in the daily hustle, having fun with friends and sharing great moments, but sometimes, small issues or miscommunications can snowball into bigger problems if they're not addressed early on. And when things go wrong, and the friendship starts to crumble, it's often because we failed to set proper boundaries along the way. These misunderstandings, trivial as they may seem at first, have the power to drive a wedge between people who once shared a deep connection. So, the lesson here is clear: never let your true friendships suffer or break down over small tantrums or missteps. If something bothers you, it's better to address it rather than let it fester until it reaches a point of no return.

Finding balance in your friendships is incredibly important. This balance isn't just about avoiding conflict or keeping things pleasant; it's about maintaining respect, trust, and a sense of mutual understanding. True friendship isn't about being constantly on the same page or agreeing on everything. It's about understanding each other's boundaries and learning how to navigate them in a way that preserves the relationship. You might think you're doing fine just going with the flow, but without clear boundaries, friendships can become imbalanced, leading to resentment or misunderstandings.

That's why it's so important to set boundaries and find a balance that works for both people. To help you with this, I've broken it down into three simple yet effective categories. These steps will make the process of setting boundaries more understandable and actionable. By taking the time to identify these areas, you can avoid potential pitfalls and make sure your friendships stay healthy and thriving, without the risk of them falling apart over small, avoidable issues. These categories will help guide you in a way that isn't just theoretical but practical, offering real steps to implement in your friendships. Let's dive into them! Here's a breakdown:

S. No	ASPECTS	DESCRIPTION	EXAMPLES	RED FLAGS
1	SELF AWARENESS	• Understanding personal boundaries, needs and values. • Recognising own emotions and triggers.	• Noticing discomfort around certain behaviours. • Recognising personal limits on socializing.	• Constantly sacrifices to please others. • Has no sense of personal boundaries.
2	CLEAR COMMUNICATION	• Expressing thoughts and boundaries openly and respectfully. • Encouraging constructive conversations.	• Sharing preferences for social plans. • Discussing concerns openly about shared living arrangements.	• Often passive-aggressive or dismissive. • Struggles to express boundaries.
3	EMPATHY	• Understanding other's feelings and perspectives. • Being open-minded about friend's views.	• Listening without interrupting. • Recognising friend's perspective before offering advice.	• Lacks compassion during tough times. • Invalidates other's feelings.

Finding Balance in Friendship vs Red Flags

SELF-AWARENESS AND REFLECTION

When it comes to cultivating meaningful and lasting friendships, one of the most important steps you can take is to understand yourself. This is a journey of introspection—taking the time to really reflect on who you are, what you value, and what you need in your relationships. It's not something that can be rushed or skipped over. Studies, such as those published in The Journal of Positive Psychology, show that individuals who are mindful of their emotional needs and who establish healthy boundaries in their friendships report significantly higher levels of satisfaction in life and stronger, more supportive connections. This doesn't just happen by chance; it's a result of actively prioritizing your well-being and understanding where your limits lie.

The first thing to do when reflecting on your relationships is to spend time with yourself. This is a moment to truly understand your feelings, without external pressures or distractions. For some people, this might be a quiet moment in the shower, while others might prefer to think deeply when they're alone, even if it's just sitting on the toilet seat. The key is to create space where you can hear your thoughts clearly. During this time, ask yourself some vital questions about your personal boundaries and emotional needs:

a) Know Your Limits

Understanding your personal limits is vital for building healthy and meaningful friendships. Take a moment to reflect: what truly brings you joy in a friendship? Is it the laughter shared during simple moments, the depth of meaningful conversations, or the adventures you experience together? Equally important, what behaviours or patterns leave you feeling uneasy or drained? Identifying these triggers is key to recognising when boundaries are being crossed.

Perhaps it's a friend who frequently demands more time or emotional support than you can comfortably give, or a situation where you're stretched thin trying to please everyone. Acknowledging these signs doesn't make you selfish—it's an essential step in prioritising your well-being. By setting clear and healthy boundaries, you create space for friendships that uplift and energise you, rather than leave you feeling overwhelmed. Boundaries aren't about shutting people out; they're about ensuring your relationships remain a source of mutual respect, balance, and happiness.

b) Prioritize Self-Care

It's also crucial to remember that it's okay to say "no" sometimes. Self-care isn't a luxury—it's a necessity. You can't be a great friend if you're not taking care of yourself first. This might mean canceling plans when you're feeling burnt out, choosing a quiet evening at home instead of going out, or being honest about your emotional capacity. The idea is to listen to your own needs and not feel guilty for setting boundaries. A friend who respects your limits will understand, and if they don't, it's worth reflecting on whether they truly value you. When you're well-rested, emotionally balanced, and at peace with yourself, you're in a much better position to be there for your friends in a genuine and supportive way.

c) Reflect on Your Needs

It's not only about recognizing your limits but also understanding what you need from your friendships. What do you value most in a friend? Is it someone who listens, someone who challenges you, or perhaps someone who is simply present during the hard times? Reflect on what you truly require in a relationship to feel supported and valued. Equally important is to identify what you can't tolerate in a friendship—whether it's dishonesty, inconsistency, or a lack of respect. Knowing these things will help you avoid unhealthy relationships and make it easier to build meaningful, fulfilling connections. Understanding your emotional needs and being clear about your expectations creates a solid foundation for your friendships to thrive.

In the end, becoming more self-aware and reflecting on your needs isn't just about ensuring your own well-being; it's about creating stronger, healthier relationships with the people around you. When you're clear about who you are and what you want, you're much more likely to attract and maintain friendships that truly enrich your life. The process of introspection might not always be easy, but it's essential for building lasting connections where both parties feel understood, respected, and supported.

LIFE EXPERIENCE:

Back in my college days, I had a moment of self-realisation during a rather challenging period in the hostel. I've always been somewhat introverted, not naturally the most social person. While I've been gradually learning to adapt, sudden changes can sometimes overwhelm me, triggering social anxiety. This was put to the test when I decided to change my roommates.

Living with people you don't entirely gel with can be tough, and over time, minor annoyances can build up into something bigger. So, when I had the opportunity to move rooms, I took it without even discussing it with my old roommates. At the time, it felt like a harsh and impulsive decision, but looking back, it was the right one. Staying would have only led to more tension and potential conflicts, which neither side deserved. That experience taught me that prioritising my mental well-being, even when it's uncomfortable, is sometimes the best choice.

CLEAR COMMUNICATION AND CONSISTENCY

Clear communication and consistency are the foundations that keep friendships strong, healthy, and resilient over time. Maya Angelou once said, "A friend may be waiting behind a stranger's face," which serves as a powerful reminder that true friendship often requires empathy and patience. It's easy to assume someone's intentions or feelings without fully understanding them, but real friends take the time to listen, learn, and adjust, even when it's difficult. Friendships thrive on clear communication, which requires not just speaking but also listening and understanding one another. Here's how we can approach building this essential foundation in our friendships:

a) Communicate Clearly

Effective communication starts with being clear about your own feelings and needs. It's essential to share what makes you comfortable and what doesn't. For example, if something bothers you—whether it's a casual comment, an action, or a habit—it's crucial to let your friend know. It doesn't mean being confrontational, but being open and honest in a non-judgmental way. When we communicate openly, it prevents misunderstandings and helps friends get to know us at a deeper level. It's also important to communicate appreciation, acknowledging when your friends make efforts to understand or support you. Good communication isn't just about sharing problems; it's about sharing joy, gratitude, and encouragement, too. When both friends make an effort to communicate clearly, it strengthens the bond and builds trust.

b) Be Assertive

Assertiveness in friendships isn't about being aggressive or forcing your opinion; it's about having the confidence to speak up for yourself and set boundaries. You have the right to express what you think and feel, even if it's uncomfortable. For example, if you need space or don't agree with something, speak up kindly but firmly. It's a delicate balance—assertiveness means standing up for yourself without disrespecting the other person. When you're assertive, you show that you value your own needs, but you also value the friendship enough to address things in a healthy manner. This means saying "no" when needed or asking for what you truly want without guilt. Strong friendships are built on mutual respect, and being assertive in a way that respects both your needs and your friend's needs will help the relationship last and grow stronger.

c) Listen Actively

One of the most important aspects of clear communication is listening. It's easy to focus on what we want to say or how we want to respond, but listening is just as vital, if not more. Active listening means giving your full attention to what the other person is saying, without distractions, interruptions, or jumping to conclusions. It's about being present in the moment and allowing your friend to feel heard and understood. When you listen with empathy, you not only learn more about your friend's thoughts and feelings but also deepen the emotional connection between you. Sometimes, friends don't need solutions; they just need someone to listen and acknowledge their experiences.

Active listening also involves asking follow-up questions, offering validation, and showing your friend that you truly care. By listening actively, you create an environment where both friends can feel supported, valued, and encouraged to be open about their lives.

In all friendships, consistency is key. It's easy to get caught up in the busyness of life and forget to check in or communicate regularly. But to build long-lasting relationships, you need to stay consistent in how you communicate, how often you reach out, and how you show up for each other. Consistency helps create a sense of security, trust, and dependability. It's about showing up in good times and bad, maintaining that emotional connection over time, and being reliable no matter what life throws your way. When both friends put effort into communication and consistency, the bond becomes unshakeable, even through life's inevitable ups and downs.

Good communication, assertiveness, and active listening don't just improve relationships—they nurture and sustain them. By mastering these skills, you not only make your friendships stronger but also contribute to a more positive and fulfilling social environment. Whether it's understanding your own needs or respecting someone else's, these principles are crucial to building long-lasting, healthy friendships that can withstand the test of time.

LIFE EXPERIENCE:

There was another pivotal moment during college when I had a minor disagreement with one of my roommates. It was a small fight, but the anger we both felt was unmistakable—a sign that a boundary had been crossed. Reflecting on it, I realised anger can serve as an important signal when something isn't right, but it has to be controlled and channelled productively.

That day, we sat down and had an honest conversation, setting clear boundaries for the future. We agreed to respect each other's space and emotions, and that understanding became the foundation for maintaining our friendship. We still shared laughs and pulled harmless pranks on each other, but from that point on, we knew not to push things too far. It was a valuable lesson in communication and the importance of setting limits with the people we care about.

EMPATHY, FLEXIBILITY AND LETTING GO

Friendships, like any meaningful relationship, require a balance of understanding, respect, and care. In order to nurture healthy, lasting friendships, it's important to cultivate qualities like empathy, flexibility, and the ability to let go when necessary. Let's break down how these elements work and why they are so crucial to maintaining strong connections with others.

a) Practice Empathy

One of the key foundations of any healthy friendship is empathy—the ability to understand and share the feelings of another person. Empathy allows you to step outside of your own perspective and put yourself in your friend's shoes. There are times when your friend may be going through a difficult time, and it's easy to feel frustrated or disconnected if you don't understand where they're coming from. However, taking a moment to reflect on how you would feel in their situation can help you approach the situation with more compassion and patience. This level of understanding not only helps you respond in a more supportive way, but it also deepens the emotional bond you share. Empathy fosters trust and makes the relationship more resilient because it shows your friend that you genuinely care about their well-being. The more you practice empathy, the stronger and more fulfilling the friendship becomes, as it's rooted in mutual care and concern.

b) Set Boundaries

While empathy and flexibility are crucial, setting boundaries in friendships is just as important. Boundaries are a way to protect your emotional health and ensure that your needs are respected within the friendship. Sometimes, friendships can become one-sided, with one person taking more than they're giving, whether it's time, emotional labor, or resources. In such cases, setting clear boundaries is essential. It's okay to say "no" if someone is asking too much of you, or if their actions are causing you stress or discomfort. Boundaries might seem difficult at first, especially if you're someone who tends to prioritize others, but they're necessary for maintaining balance. When you set healthy boundaries, you're not only protecting yourself but also ensuring that the friendship remains respectful and equal. Boundaries can be physical, emotional, or even time-related, depending on what works for you. By being honest about your limits and communicating them effectively, you help foster an environment of mutual respect, where both parties can thrive.

c) Know When to Let Go

Friendships are meant to enrich our lives, but sometimes they can become unhealthy or draining. If you've tried setting boundaries and practicing empathy but the friendship continues to cause you stress, disappointment, or hurt, it may be time to evaluate whether it's worth continuing. Letting go of a friendship is never easy, especially if you've invested a lot of time and energy into it, but it's crucial to recognize when a relationship no longer serves a positive purpose in your life. If someone consistently crosses the boundaries you've set, or if their behavior becomes toxic or emotionally abusive, it might be necessary to distance yourself or even end the friendship altogether. Letting go can be difficult, but it's an important step toward self-care. It's essential to surround yourself with people who make you feel valued, supported, and happy. As Paulo Coelho beautifully wrote in The Alchemist, "When someone leaves, it's because someone else is about to arrive." This insight reminds us that letting go of one friendship can create space for new, more fulfilling relationships to enter our lives. It's okay to outgrow friendships, and by letting go, you open the door for new connections that align better with your current needs and values.

In conclusion, friendships require ongoing effort and self-awareness. Empathy helps you connect, flexibility allows you to adjust to changes, and knowing when to let go helps you protect your emotional health. By nurturing these qualities, you can build strong, meaningful friendships that bring joy and support into your life while maintaining the boundaries necessary for your well-being.

LIFE EXPERIENCE:

Relationships often come with their own share of highs and lows, but one of the most profound lessons I've learned is how to let go gracefully. I think about my relationship with Ala, someone who was such an important part of my life. While many of my friends have experienced bitter, messy breakups, I feel incredibly fortunate that Ala and I had a smooth, mutual parting.

Even though our romantic relationship ended, we remained friends. In fact, just this month, in December 2024, Ala told me about her upcoming wedding in February 2025. I'm genuinely happy for her and plan to attend the ceremony, bringing a thoughtful gift to celebrate her new chapter.

Our story is a testament to the power of empathy and mutual respect. We both recognised that certain disagreements made it impossible to continue as a couple, but we valued our connection enough to let go without bitterness. That kind of flexibility and willingness to prioritise understanding over resentment is what has kept our friendship alive, and I hope it will last a lifetime.

CHAPTER FIVE

HOW TO LET GO

Psychologist Dr. Henry Cloud, in '*Boundaries*', says, "You get what you tolerate." This stresses the importance of clearly defining and communicating what you can and cannot accept in relationships. The book, originally published in 1992, has been updated and expanded over the years to address new challenges in the digital age, with the latest edition released in 2017 by Zondervan.

Stephen R. Covey, in '*The 7 Habits of Highly Effective People*' published in 1989, says, "You have to decide what your highest priorities are and have the courage—pleasantly, smilingly, non-apologetically—to say 'no' to other things." Covey emphasizes the importance of setting priorities and confidently saying "no" to distractions to focus on one's highest goals. His advice is encapsulated in the concept of "Put First Things First," which is Habit 3 in his framework. This habit encourages readers to prioritize tasks based on importance rather than urgency, a practice he believes leads to more meaningful and effective life management.

Melody Beattie, a pioneer in the field of self-help, is well-known for her insights on codependency, particularly in her influential 1986 book '*Codependent No More*'. she introduced the concept of codependency and emphasized the importance of setting boundaries as a form of self-care. Beattie encourages individuals to recognize feelings of discomfort or hurt as cues to reevaluate their boundaries, an idea that has resonated with many readers over the years. Beattie revisited and expanded these ideas in The New Codependency, published in 2009, where she updated her perspective for a modern audience. This book provides additional guidance on differentiating between healthy and codependent behaviors, and it reinforces her view that maintaining clear boundaries is essential for mental well-being. According to Beattie, self-care and boundary-setting are crucial for breaking free from patterns that can lead to unhealthy, codependent relationships.

Sometimes, no matter how much effort we pour into something—whether it's making compromises, changing ourselves, or finding creative solutions—it just doesn't seem to work out the way we hoped. We hold on tightly, believing that with enough dedication, we can mend what's broken or create something better. We tell ourselves that things will improve, that it's just a matter of time, patience, or understanding. And so, we try again and again, giving it our best shot. But despite all the effort, sometimes the situation remains unchanged, or worse, starts to feel even more strained. It's like pouring water into a cup with a crack—it leaks no matter how much you try to refill it.

When this happens, the best course of action is often to step back and give things some breathing room. Taking a break doesn't mean giving up; it means allowing yourself and the other person space to reflect, reset, and gain clarity. Sometimes, distance can provide perspective and help both sides see things in a new light. It might even lead to the realization that the issues weren't as big as they seemed, or it could spark a renewed effort to work things out. However, there are also times when even a break doesn't change the underlying problems, and despite every attempt, things just don't get better.

In such cases, it might be a sign that it's time to let go. Letting go isn't easy—it's painful and feels like admitting defeat. But it's not about failing; it's about recognizing when something isn't serving your well-being or happiness anymore. Holding on too tightly can sometimes hurt more than walking away. By letting go, you're giving both yourself and the other person the opportunity to find peace and growth separately. It's an act of self-respect and compassion, even if it feels like a loss in the moment. In the long run, making the choice to move on can open doors to new possibilities, healthier connections, and a sense of freedom that comes from putting yourself first.

Ultimately, life is about balance—knowing when to hold on and fight for something worth keeping and recognizing when it's time to release it with grace. Letting go doesn't erase the good memories or diminish the effort you put in. Instead, it honors the journey you've been on and clears the way for what's next. It's a bittersweet but necessary part of growth, teaching us that sometimes the healthiest and most loving choice we can make is to walk away.

STRATEGY	KEY TAKEAWAYS	EXAMPLES
Gradual Shifts to a Casual Friendship	Gradually reduce frequency of contact and intensity of relationship	Instead of daily charts, reduce to weekly check-ins
Communicate Honestly and Kindness	Use 'I' statements and focus on personal needs	"I'm focusing on my personal goals right now"
Leave the Door Open for Future Reconnection	End on a positive note and express openness to future connection	"I'll look forward to catching up when the timing is right"

A Framework for fading a Friendship

GRADUAL SHIFT

Opt for a Gradual Shift to a Casual Friendship

Aristotle's famous quote, "*Wishing to be friends is quick work, but friendship is a slow ripening fruit,*" reflects his view on the enduring and gradual nature of true friendship. This line emphasizes that genuine friendships, unlike quick acquaintances, take time to deepen and mature. Aristotle discussed this concept in his works, such as the 'Nicomachean Ethics', where he explored how meaningful friendships evolve through shared experiences, mutual respect, and understanding. This notion suggests that friendships can experience natural ebbs and flows without necessarily needing drastic breaks, as true connections can withstand the test of time and adversity.

Opting for a gradual shift toward a casual friendship is often the most natural and least confrontational approach when you feel the dynamics of a relationship need to change. It allows both parties to adjust without the drama or hurt feelings that can accompany a sudden break. This method relies on subtle shifts in your interactions and can help preserve the positive aspects of your connection while easing out of the more intense or time-consuming elements of the friendship.

One effective way to make this transition is by gradually reducing how often you meet up or chat. If you're used to catching up every weekend, for example, you could start spreading those meet-ups out to once a month or every few weeks. The key is to do this naturally, without drawing attention to the change. Instead of actively avoiding your friend, focus on filling your time with other commitments, hobbies, or social groups. This helps create a sense of balance and lets the friendship organically settle into a less intense rhythm.

Another strategy is to prioritize group settings over one-on-one hangouts. If you share the same social circle or live in close proximity—like being flatmates or part of a community group—group gatherings can be a perfect way to maintain a friendly connection without the pressure of individual attention. Attending parties, social events, or even casual group dinners shifts the focus from the two of you to the broader group dynamic. This not only lightens the emotional load but also provides opportunities to bond without the same level of intensity as before.

You might also subtly redirect conversations or activities to avoid revisiting topics that once formed the foundation of a deeper connection. Instead of diving into personal or emotional topics, stick to lighter, more casual subjects. Over time, this shift in tone can help redefine the relationship in a way that feels natural and comfortable for both of you.

By taking this gradual approach, you allow the friendship to evolve rather than end abruptly. It's a way of saying, "I still value you, but I need to create some space," without ever having to say those words outright. This kind of soft transition is particularly helpful in situations where you still care about the person but feel the need to realign your priorities or boundaries. It's less about cutting ties and more about finding a new balance, one that fits better with where you are in life. In the end, it leaves the door open for occasional reconnections and ensures that the positive memories and mutual respect remain intact.

LIFE EXPERIENCE:

There are times when friendships evolve, and distancing yourself becomes necessary, as in the case of my acquaintance, Kushal Sharma. We initially met through work, collaborating on a mutual task that brought us together despite being from different companies. Over time, our working relationship blossomed into a genuine friendship, and we began meeting outside of professional settings.

However, things changed when Kushal started introducing me to his group of friends who engaged in habits like dry smoking and sneezing powder—activities I was uncomfortable with. While I valued our friendship, I realised that this environment wasn't right for me. Abruptly cutting ties felt harsh and potentially harmful, both for Bishal and his friends. Instead, I decided on a gradual approach, meeting him less often and slowly creating distance. It allowed both of us to adjust without causing unnecessary friction.

HONEST COMMUNICATION

Communicate Honestly with Kindness

Harriet Lerner's seminal book *'The Dance of Anger'*, first published in 1985 by Harper & Row, delves deeply into the nuances of anger, particularly as it manifests in women's relationships. It's not just a book about managing anger; it's about understanding its role as a signal for change and growth in interpersonal dynamics. Lerner explores the societal pressures and internalized expectations that often make it difficult for women to express their anger openly. She emphasizes that anger, when approached constructively, can be a powerful tool for creating healthier, more authentic relationships. Through practical advice and real-world examples, she teaches readers how to use clear communication and self-awareness to navigate conflicts and assert their needs without fear of rejection or guilt. By fostering honest dialogue and staying true to one's feelings, Lerner argues, individuals can cultivate stronger, more fulfilling connections. The book's timeless insights have cemented its place as a cornerstone in both psychology and the self-help genre, offering guidance not just on anger, but on boundaries, self-respect, and emotional well-being.

When it comes to navigating the delicate process of stepping back from a close friendship, Lerner's principles of honesty and clarity can be invaluable. A gentle, empathetic approach is essential to maintain respect and minimize hurt feelings. If your friend senses a change and asks about it, focusing on your own needs rather than their behavior is often the most compassionate way to handle the conversation. For instance, you might say something like, "I've been dedicating more time to my personal goals lately" or "I'm working through some things in my own life and need a little space." By framing the explanation around your personal journey, you avoid assigning blame and create a space for understanding.

Another effective way to ease the transition is by using "I" statements, which emphasize your perspective without placing fault on the other person. Saying something like, "I've been feeling the need for more alone time recently" or "I'm trying to focus on my own growth right now" makes the conversation about your internal process rather than their actions. This subtle but crucial shift in language helps to keep the dialogue constructive and avoids making them feel criticized or rejected.

It's important to approach the situation with kindness and clarity. Acknowledge the value of the friendship and express gratitude for the bond you've shared. For example, you might say, "Our friendship means a lot to me, and I hope you know how much I value the memories we've created." By reinforcing the positive aspects of the relationship, you help ensure the other person feels appreciated, even if things are changing. This approach not only softens the impact of the conversation but also increases the likelihood that the friendship can adapt to its new dynamic without unnecessary tension or resentment.

Stepping back from a friendship doesn't always mean the connection is lost forever. Life circumstances often change, and relationships evolve as a result. By being honest, gentle, and focused on your own needs, you create an environment where mutual respect and understanding can thrive. In doing so, you honor the friendship while also prioritizing your personal growth, ensuring the transition is as smooth and respectful as possible for both parties.

LIFE EXPERIENCE:

Honesty, paired with kindness, can work wonders in delicate situations. Some months later, Bishal faced a personal tragedy—his mother passed away. Since his mother had known me, I felt it was important to visit and console him during this difficult time. It was during these visits that he opened up about realising the negative influence his friends had on him. My support, coupled with our honest conversations, helped him gradually distance himself from that group.

This experience reaffirmed how effective communication can be. Many people, driven by ego or reluctance, avoid addressing sensitive matters, and relationships end up breaking down entirely. But when approached with empathy, even strained relationships can be repaired or strengthened.

FUTURE RECONNECTION

Leave the Door Open for Future Reconnection

Brené Brown's book *'The Gifts of Imperfection'*, published in 2010, delves deeply into themes that resonate with anyone seeking to live a more authentic and fulfilling life. The book emphasizes self-acceptance, vulnerability, and the importance of setting healthy boundaries. Brown, a celebrated research professor and expert on topics like shame and vulnerability, presents these ideas in a way that feels both academic and personal. Her central message is that living authentically—what she calls "wholehearted living"—requires embracing imperfection and showing ourselves the same kindness we often extend to others.

One of the book's key takeaways is the idea that setting boundaries is not just a practical tool but a profound act of self-love. For Brown, boundaries are a way to protect our energy and emotional well-being, even when it might upset others. She famously writes, "Daring to set boundaries is about having the courage to love ourselves, even when we risk disappointing others." This quote encapsulates her belief that prioritizing self-respect is essential for emotional health and personal growth. Boundaries are not walls but bridges that connect us to our values and allow us to engage with others from a place of integrity and self-worth.

When navigating friendships or any relationship, Brown's insights on boundaries can be particularly valuable. Sometimes, we might feel the need to take a step back, and that's perfectly okay. If life circumstances require some distance, there's a compassionate way to handle it. Ending a conversation or interaction on a warm note can leave the door open for future connection. For example, saying something like, "I'll look forward to catching up when the timing is right!" communicates care while honoring your own needs. It's a way of maintaining the relationship without feeling pressured or overwhelmed.

Understanding that both you and your friend are on unique journeys can help alleviate guilt or anxiety about taking a step back. Life is full of twists and turns, and sometimes friendships need room to breathe. This doesn't necessarily mean an ending; it might simply be a pause. Time apart can offer both people an opportunity to grow individually, which can strengthen the bond when paths cross again. Often, relationships that have had the space to evolve naturally become richer and more meaningful when you reconnect.

Leaving things open-ended, without resentment or finality, can be a powerful way to honor the relationship's history and potential. It allows for flexibility and hope, making future interactions feel fresh rather than weighed down by unresolved emotions. As Brown suggests, living authentically and with self-respect often means making tough but necessary choices, and sometimes those choices include redefining how we engage with the people in our lives. This doesn't diminish the connection; instead, it can create the foundation for a deeper, more balanced relationship in the future.

LIFE EXPERIENCE:

Sometimes, friendships don't end—they pause, leaving room for future understanding. Although I haven't personally experienced this, I recall a memorable incident involving two of my college batchmates, Dinanka and Abhinash.

On the very first day of college, both of them had a heated argument that escalated into a full-blown fight—right in front of the Principal's office, no less! The commotion erupted while we were queued up to submit our documents, and it became the talk of the campus. One of them was from my hostel, while the other lived in a different one, so I inevitably heard both sides of the story. It turned out that their fight stemmed from a trivial misunderstanding.

Fortunately, neither of them held onto grudges. Instead, they chose to sit down, share their perspectives, and clear the air. Over time, they grew to become not just cordial but genuinely good friends. Imagine how different their college years would have been if they had allowed that one incident to define their relationship.

CHAPTER SIX

PERSONAL ALIBIS

Back in my engineering days, I met Ala during our college's annual fest. It was one of those moments when you meet someone, and the connection feels effortless right from the start. There was something about her energy that just clicked with mine. We were both part of the same group, but there was a sense of familiarity and ease between us, even though we hadn't spent much time together before. From the beginning, it wasn't like the typical friendships you see, filled with forced pleasantries or awkward silences. It just felt natural, like we had known each other for a long time.

We had a smooth relationship overall—no major fights, no dramatic disagreements. Our bond was comfortable, and we just worked together. Ala had this calm, steady energy that balanced my slightly more rigid, routine-driven nature. I was someone who loved structure—planning my days down to the minute, following a set routine. She, on the other hand, was more spontaneous, open to whatever life threw her way. But somehow, these differences didn't cause friction. They complemented each other. She kept me from getting too rigid, and I helped bring some order to her otherwise chaotic life.

Fast forward to 2017, after college, and life seemed to align perfectly for us. Both of us landed jobs in Guwahati—Ala as a university counselor and me at a marketing company. With our careers just starting to take off, we made the decision to share a flat. The excitement of setting up a new home, navigating the challenges of adulthood, and supporting each other in our new roles felt like the perfect continuation of what we had started during college. For the first year, everything felt perfect. Living together was exciting and comfortable. We balanced each other's quirks, supported one another, and it genuinely felt like we were building a life as a team.

However, as time passed, we started to change. I found myself drawn to a more structured lifestyle. Yoga, morning runs, healthy eating—I was becoming the person who found peace in a well-organized, predictable day. My routine began to revolve around my personal growth, something that became important to me as I started to focus on long-term goals. My mornings followed a strict pattern—waking up early, going for a run at dawn, having breakfast at the same time every day. Bedtime was just as consistent; early nights meant early mornings. It was a rhythm that kept me grounded.

Ala, on the other hand, started embracing her free-spirited side more than ever. While I thrived on consistency, she thrived in the chaos. Her nights were often late, not just spent partying, but also working on her projects or simply enjoying the quiet solitude the night offered. Weekends became her time for adventure—Saturday night-outs with friends, spontaneous plans, and a schedule that was completely unpredictable. While I had no problem with her doing what made her happy, the disparity between our lifestyles started to create subtle friction.

At first, our differences were manageable. I was still able to stick to my routines, and she was able to live her life without too much interference. But soon, these differences started to manifest in ways that I couldn't ignore. Ala began hosting Saturday night parties at our flat. It wasn't just a casual get-together; it was a full-on event. Friends, music, drinks, and a lot of energy. EDM blasting through the speakers, people laughing and talking loudly—it was her version of fun. I wasn't much of a drinker and had no interest in partying, but I found myself joining in, thinking it would help me fit in better. It was a way to bond, I convinced myself. However, I never truly felt at ease. I was sitting on the sidelines, feeling out of place while everyone around me was caught up in the excitement. Over time, these nights became more frequent, and my friends started to invite me out after work for similar gatherings. The pressure to fit in grew. I didn't want to be the odd one out, so I joined in, even though I didn't feel like myself.

The more I gave in to the pressure to keep up with these events, the more I began to lose touch with my own needs and routines. My morning runs became sporadic, my healthy eating habits fell apart, and I started to feel a deep sense of disconnect from myself. I was exhausted—not just physically, but emotionally too. It was as if I had stopped listening to my body and started living for everyone else. It felt like I was losing sight of who I had worked so hard to become. I was tired, drained, and restless. The person I used to be—the person who thrived on structure and routine—seemed to be slipping away.

Ala, being her perceptive self, noticed the change. One evening, after a particularly tough week, she pulled out a bottle of scotch and sat me down for a heart-to-heart. I don't know what prompted her to do it, but it was exactly what I needed. She didn't bombard me with questions or tell me what to do. Instead, she just listened. And as I began to talk, I realized how much I had been carrying—how much of myself I had sacrificed to keep everyone happy. Over drinks, I opened up to her in a way I hadn't done in a long time. I told her how I felt disconnected from my own life, how I was exhausted from trying to fit into a mold that wasn't mine. I confessed how hard it was for me to say no, to disappoint people, to create boundaries.

Ala listened patiently, nodding, offering her perspective when needed, but mostly letting me pour my heart out. When I was done, she looked at me with a mixture of concern and understanding. "You're a people-pleaser," she said, her voice gentle but firm. "You're always putting others first, trying to make sure everyone's happy—even when it costs you your own peace. You need to stop that, for your sake."

Her words hit me hard, but in a way that was exactly what I needed to hear. She went on to explain how important it was to set boundaries—not just with others, but with myself. Setting boundaries wasn't about shutting people out or being selfish; it was about making room for what truly mattered. She told me that I needed to prioritize my own needs sometimes, even if it meant disappointing others. And this wasn't just something that applied to friends and work—it applied to our relationship as well. She reminded me that our different lifestyles didn't have to cause friction. It was possible for us to coexist in a way that respected each other's choices. We didn't have to live the same way, but we had to find a middle ground, a place where we could both thrive without compromising our individual needs.

That conversation marked a turning point for me. It wasn't a magical fix—there were still challenges to overcome, and there were still moments when our differences caused tension. But Ala's honesty and support helped me regain a sense of balance. I learned to speak up when I needed space, to stick to my routines when they mattered, and to compromise without losing myself. I realized that relationships didn't need to be free of conflict to be strong. What mattered most was how we communicated, how we understood each other, and how we respected each other's boundaries.

Looking back, I feel incredibly fortunate to have had Ala by my side during that time. She didn't just help me navigate through a rough patch; she taught me how to embrace differences and build a life that felt true to myself. In a way, she helped me see that it's okay to be different, to have separate needs and desires, but that doesn't mean those differences have to break us apart. If anything, they can make us stronger, as long as we communicate openly and with respect. Life isn't about perfect harmony, but about finding a balance that works for both people. And in the end, that balance is what made our relationship work, and what continues to shape our friendship to this day.

After spending 5-6 months engaging in what I like to call "self-discovery sessions" with her, I emerged as a transformed person. These months weren't just about getting to know myself better—they were about learning what I now consider the ultimate life skill: the Alibi, or as we fondly call it in Hindi, Bahana (बहाना). This isn't just a skill—it's an art form, a way to navigate the complexities of social obligations and personal desires. It's the reason behind this book's title. Over time, I've refined and perfected my alibi game, and I'm about to share some of my most effective strategies with you. The key to a solid alibi is simplicity, believability, and just the right amount of conviction to make it work without raising any suspicions. So let's dive right in, starting with the ultimate tool in any alibi arsenal: the white lie.

The Art of the White Lie (सफेद झूठ)

We've all heard the saying, "A little white lie never hurt anyone," and honestly, there's truth to that. A well-placed, harmless fib can be the difference between an awkward situation and a smooth exit. Whether you're trying to avoid an uncomfortable family gathering or gracefully bowing out of an event you'd rather not attend, a simple lie can save you from unwanted interactions. But here's the catch—relying on the same old excuses like "I'm busy" or "I'm feeling sick" eventually loses its charm. People catch on, and suddenly your usual lines start sounding less believable. That's when you need to get creative. You need to level up your alibi game. And believe me, I've got some tried-and-true white lies that have been my go-to for years. Let me share a few.

RELIGION-BASED ALIBIS

ReReligion-Based Alibis: Best for Indians

In a diverse and culturally rich country like India, religion can be your greatest ally when crafting excuses. The beauty of this type of alibi lies in its universal understanding.

People don't question religious practices easily, and when you use it as a reason to decline an invitation or avoid a social event, it's nearly impossible to challenge. I've often found myself saying, "I'm avoiding alcohol and non-veg this month due to a religious vow," and let me tell you, it works like a charm every single time. And the best part? If anyone dares to get too persistent, I simply flip the script and ask, "Why don't you join me in observing the restrictions of your own beliefs?" This tactic, especially in smaller towns or Tier 2 cities, is not only effective but often leaves people speechless.

Here are a few more religion-based excuses that I've personally relied on and can confidently say they work wonders:

"I've taken a vow to avoid alcohol and non-veg for a while."

"There's a puja at home today, like the Narayani Puja."

"It's Ekadasi, so I'm fasting or avoiding certain foods today."

"Today is the death anniversary of my grandparent, so I'm staying in for the rituals."

What makes these excuses so foolproof is their simplicity. They're easy to remember, culturally relevant, and most importantly, they're almost impossible to argue with. There's something about tying your excuse to a sacred or meaningful cultural practice that gives it an undeniable authenticity. Even in cosmopolitan cities like Mumbai or Delhi, where people are generally more open-minded, this excuse remains hard to question. The key to pulling it off is to keep your explanation short and sweet—don't over-explain, because the more details you offer, the more suspicious it sounds. Just a firm, well-timed excuse, and you'll find yourself navigating the situation with ease.

Why This Works So Well?

The reason religion-based excuses are so effective is simple: they tap into a universal cultural sentiment—respect for religious and cultural practices. People may not follow the same customs, but most will respect and understand them. There's an inherent layer of empathy that comes with acknowledging someone's beliefs, which is why these excuses work so well in almost every social setting. Whether you're dealing with family, friends, or colleagues, the respect for cultural values creates an immediate layer of authenticity. The beauty of this tactic lies in its ability to be flexible. Whether it's a fasting day, a prayer ritual, or a simple vow, it's hard to argue with someone who is 'honoring their faith.'

This approach is subtle and doesn't require much effort. The more you speak with confidence and conviction, the better it works. Don't elaborate. Just say your piece, nod politely, and move on. The less you try to justify it, the more legitimate it sounds.

The Secret to Crafting a Perfect Alibi

While religion-based alibis are a staple, they are just the beginning of the alibi toolkit. Over the years, I've learned that adaptability and creativity are the keys to a truly great alibi. Religion-based excuses work in certain contexts, but for other situations, I've had to get more creative. The trick lies in understanding the nature of the event you're trying to avoid, and crafting an excuse that fits seamlessly into that situation. Sometimes it's about timing—other times it's about delivering your excuse with the right mix of casualness and conviction. The more natural your excuse feels, the more likely people are to accept it without a second thought.

As we move forward, I'll be sharing more creative and foolproof strategies that I've refined over the years. These tricks are born out of trial and error, but most importantly, they work. Whether you're trying to get out of a social gathering, skip out on an obligation, or simply need a little extra time for yourself, these alibis will help you navigate the trickier moments of life. So, stay tuned, because in the next chapter, I'll be revealing the other creative alibi tools that I use regularly and which have never let me down.

But for now, remember: The art of the alibi isn't just about coming up with clever excuses—it's about understanding the subtle dance of human interaction. It's about knowing how to say the right thing at the right time, with just the right amount of sincerity. It's not about lying to hurt anyone—it's about creating a space where you can be true to yourself while maintaining respect and consideration for those around you. The white lie, particularly when used sparingly and thoughtfully, can be an incredibly powerful tool in achieving that balance. So go ahead, practice your alibis, and next time you need a graceful exit, you'll know exactly what to say.

EXCUSE	SAMPLE STATEMENT	WHY IT WORKS	INTENSITY
DIETRY VOW	"I'm avoiding alcohol and non-veg this week."	"If friends are not too pushy, they would understand healthy living."	MILD
VOW DUE TO RELIGIOUS BELIEF	"I've taken a vow to avoid alcohol due to regional Puja"	"A personal vow in a religious context is often respected without question."	MODERATE
SPECIFIC FASTING DAY	"Today is Ekadadi etc, so I'm off certain foods."	"Many in India observe fasting days as per their belief."	HIGH
RELIGIOUS CEREMONY AT HOME	"There's a Narayani/Govardhan Puja at home."	"This, which is commonly understood to be of regional cultural importance."	VERY HIGH
DEATH ANNIVERSARY OF FAMILY MEMBER	"It's relative's death anniversary."	"This is a somber excuse that people are reluctant to challenge."	EXTREMELY HIGH

Religious and Cultural Alibis for Avoiding Social Commitments

HEALTH ISSUES ALIBIS

Health Issues Alibis: A Universal Ace

Health-based excuses have become a go-to strategy, especially when you're navigating friendships or social situations with people who follow a more modern, Westernized mindset. Let's be honest—when you try to opt out of something using the excuse of cultural or religious obligations, it's often met with varying degrees of skepticism or confusion, depending on the group you're dealing with. But health? Now that's a whole different ball game. Health-related excuses are universally accepted, not just because they're rooted in something people can relate to, but because no one wants to appear inconsiderate or dismissive of someone's well-being. It's like using a trump card in a social setting—who's going to question your doctor's advice or a legitimate health concern? It's a foolproof way of gracefully stepping out of situations you'd rather avoid.

One of my go-to health excuses is something like, "I'm on a strict diet because of my fatty liver." It's straightforward, serious enough to avoid further questions, and leaves no room for awkward follow-ups. When you say it with a tone of slight seriousness but not melodrama, it often elicits a sympathetic response, and the conversation moves on smoothly without anyone pressing for details. But it's not just about what you say—it's about how you say it. For example, adding a touch of relatability can make the excuse even more believable. You can say something like, "I went a bit overboard at a wedding last month, and my health report didn't look great." By casually mentioning an overindulgent past event, you humanize the excuse, making it sound even more understandable and real.

The beauty of health-related excuses is in their versatility. Over the years, I've come up with a few variations, all effective in different settings. For example, "I'm focusing on my diet to shed some belly fat" works like a charm, especially in fitness-conscious circles. Everyone appreciates a bit of self-discipline, and some may even cheer you on. Another one I like is "My stomach's been acting up recently." It's vague but universally relatable. Stomach issues are something almost everyone has dealt with, so people are usually understanding and won't press you for specifics. On days when I feel like pulling out the big guns, I'll say, "My last test showed a fatty liver." It's direct enough to sound legitimate, but not alarmingly serious to make people worry.

For situations when I need something that sounds simple and universally understood, "I've got heartburn from acidity" works every time. Heartburn is a common complaint, and it's one of those issues that doesn't come with a stigma. It's just something people deal with from time to time, so no one is going to question you. If I'm in the mood for an excuse that sounds more serious but still won't invite probing questions, I'll use "My doctor thinks it might be a stomach ulcer." An ulcer is a well-understood issue, and most people are reluctant to ask more about it for fear of seeming inconsiderate or invasive.

Why This Works So Well

What makes health excuses so particularly effective is their ability to shut down conversations without offending anyone. Unlike other types of excuses, which can sometimes sound dismissive or defensive, health-related justifications tend to evoke empathy and concern. This means that people are far less likely to challenge your choices or push for more information. They recognize that health is personal, and they want to be respectful of your boundaries. Additionally, health excuses are incredibly adaptable. Whether you're skipping out on a meal you don't want to eat, avoiding an event you're not in the mood for, or explaining why you prefer a quieter lifestyle, these excuses work in almost any social context.

And here's the secret weapon—overexplaining just a little. It might sound counterintuitive, but adding a bit more context to your excuse can make it even more compelling. For instance, saying something like, "I've been trying to cut back on fried foods because my cholesterol levels were borderline last time I checked" sounds responsible and medically sound. This type of detail conveys that you're being proactive about your health, making it even harder for someone to question your decision. It's like giving your excuse extra weight, making it not only plausible but also responsible.

In many ways, health-based excuses not only serve as a shield to protect your boundaries but also help to establish you as someone who's mindful of their well-being. They allow you to navigate social situations without offending anyone, all while maintaining control over your personal space and choices. And let's face it—there's something quietly empowering about taking charge of your health and being able to politely decline invitations or activities that don't align with your current needs. When you strategically use health as your excuse, you can subtly shift the conversation in your favor, creating an atmosphere where people respect your decisions rather than challenging them.

What's truly powerful about health-based excuses is how they balance personal and impersonal. They feel personal because they're about your body and your well-being, but they also keep a certain level of distance. You're offering enough information to make your excuse believable, but you're not opening the door for endless questioning. It's the perfect sweet spot between being honest and maintaining privacy. This blend of transparency without vulnerability is what makes health excuses so effective.

In today's fast-paced world, where everyone is trying to juggle countless priorities, using health-related reasons as an excuse can work to your advantage. It's not just about getting out of a situation—it's about earning respect while doing so. When you prioritise your health, people tend to admire your discipline and self-awareness, even if they don't fully understand the details. It sends a message that you value yourself and are willing to take the steps needed to maintain your well-being. In a way, it positions you as responsible and thoughtful, qualities that often earn admiration.

Health-related excuses also provide a way to navigate tricky social situations with grace. Whether it's skipping a late-night event, avoiding indulgent foods, or taking time to recharge, these excuses are almost universally accepted and rarely questioned. They allow you to bow out without feeling awkward or rude, offering a relatable reason that most people will respect.

At their core, these excuses aren't just about avoidance; they're about asserting your boundaries and putting your well-being first. They might not solve every social dilemma, but they can help you navigate many with ease and confidence. When used thoughtfully, they're a powerful tool for maintaining balance in your life—showing that sometimes, saying no is the most respectful thing you can do for yourself and others.

EXCUSE	SAMPLE STATEMENT	WHY IT WORKS	INTENSITY
DIET FOCUS	"I'm focusing on my diet to shed some belly fat."	Diet goals are common and relatable.	LOW
STOMACH UPSET	"My stomach's been acting up recently."	No one wants to risk making it worse.	MODERATE
FATTY LIVER DIAGNOSIS	"My last test showed a fatty up recently."	Medical issue feels serious and discourages pushing.	HIGH
HEARTBURN/ACIDITY	"I've got heartburn from acidity."	Quite serious and hard to argue against.	VERY HIGH
PROBABLE STOMACH ULCER	"My doctor warned me of probable stomach ulcer."	"Sounds serious and people will naturally suggest taking care."	EXTREMELY HIGH

Health Alibis for Avoiding Social Commitments

REAL-LIFE MOMENT

A REAL-LIFE MOMENT OF SAYING 'NO' TO 11 PERSISTENT OFFICE MATES:

It was October, my birthday month—a time I always associate with fresh starts and personal growth. This year, I resolved to go on a 'clean' streak: no junk food, no alcohol, and nothing indulgent. Just wholesome living for the entire month. It felt like a perfect challenge, a way to test my discipline and start the new year of my life on the right foot. But fate, as it often does, had other plans.

That same October, Diwali rolled around, and my office colleagues decided to celebrate with a grand dinner party. It was a festive, glittering occasion, brimming with camaraderie and indulgence. The timing was almost poetic—it felt like the universe was testing my resolve.

CASE 1: Three Colleagues Try to Persuade Me

At first, it was just three colleagues trying to convince me to join the party. They were all younger than me, playful and persuasive, making the idea of just "one cheat day" sound like no big deal. It left me with two choices:

OPTION 1: **Say YES** – It was tempting. After all, one day wouldn't undo weeks of effort, right? I could enjoy the laughter, the food, and the drinks, and then get back on track the very next day. But deeper down, I knew there was more at stake:

Consequence A: Breaking My Self-Promise – This wasn't just about food; it was about integrity. I had set a personal goal, and giving in felt like betraying my own commitment.

Consequence B: Losing Credibility – If I said 'yes' now, they might think I was easily swayed. And in the future, their attempts to persuade me might become even more relentless, thinking I'd eventually cave every time.

OPTION 2: **Say NO** – Refusing would keep my streak alive and reinforce my self-discipline. Sure, they might see me as "boring" in the moment, but later, they'd respect my determination. More importantly, I'd respect myself.

So, I said a polite "no," dodging the temptation with a smile.

CASE 2: Senior Colleagues Join In

Soon enough, three senior colleagues entered the picture, determined to change my mind. Now, these were older, more authoritative figures, and saying "no" to them wasn't as easy as brushing off my peers. Their arguments were layered with humor and a touch of authority, making it harder to hold my ground.

But I had a plan. With a straight face, I said, "I've been having some stomach issues lately, so I think it's better to avoid heavy food." Senior colleagues, seasoned by life's trials, immediately understood the universal horror of digestive troubles. While they weren't thrilled, they let it slide with a few understanding nods and pats on my back.

CASE 3: The Girls Brigade, Led by Oshin

As if the universe wasn't done testing me, four of my female colleagues, including Oshin—my old college crush—decided to try their hand at persuasion. They came armed with charm and determination, giggling and joking as they tried to coax me into attending.

For a moment, I felt my resolve waver. Oshin's playful teasing hit a nostalgic nerve. But then, I remembered Zakir Khan's iconic mantra: "#SakhtLaunda" (A Firm Lad). I smiled and gently, but firmly, refused. It was a small victory, one that felt like a personal milestone in standing my ground without being rude.

CASE 4: The Senior Manager's Call

The final challenge came the day before the party, in the form of a phone call from my senior manager. Now, this was tricky—he was not just my boss but also something of a mentor, someone I deeply respected. Turning him down felt almost impossible.

So, I brought out my best excuse: "The doctor thinks I might have a gastric ulcer. Better safe than sorry, right?" That did the trick. He immediately encouraged me to skip the party and focus on my health. Crisis averted.

That's how I navigated the social minefield of a Diwali dinner party while staying true to my goals. Each interaction left me a little more confident in saying "no" when it mattered.

But life has a way of balancing victories with lessons. In the years that followed, these moments of discipline and self-prioritization sometimes created distance between me and my friends. By 2020, when the lockdowns began, that distance had grown. While they explored quarantine trends like Dalgona coffee and midnight calls, I stuck to my routines. Calls went unanswered; texts became less frequent.

By the time normalcy returned, things had changed. We were back in Guwahati in 2022, but our dynamics weren't the same. Little misunderstandings crept in, and while there was never a major fallout, by 2023, we amicably decided to go our separate ways.

Sometimes, life's tests teach us more than we realize in the moment. Looking back, I cherish the lessons those October days taught me—not just about discipline, but about navigating relationships and staying true to myself.

Conclusion

Reflecting on this journey, I find myself deeply appreciating the profound impact my time with Ala has had on me. Looking back, it's clear just how different we were—her carefree, free-spirited nature versus my need for structure and routine. Despite these stark differences, our relationship was one of the most meaningful and rewarding chapters of my life. We were able to find common ground, and it was that space between our differences where the magic of our connection truly blossomed. Even when things changed and we reached the point of parting ways, the decision wasn't filled with animosity or regret. Instead, it was a mutual understanding, rooted in respect for each other's journeys. And, perhaps most importantly, we continue to share a friendship, a testament to the strength and maturity of the bond we once had.

Through Ala, I learned valuable lessons about balance and boundaries, lessons that will stay with me long after this phase of my life. She taught me that setting boundaries isn't about shutting others out or building walls—it's about creating space for the things that truly matter. It's about knowing when to say yes and when to say no, not out of fear, but out of a deep respect for your own needs and values. Relationships, especially friendships, are delicate and unique. Not all of them are meant to last forever, and that's okay. Some people come into our lives for a season, and even though their time with us may be brief, they leave a lasting imprint on our hearts.

I've shared these experiences not as a set of rules to follow but as personal reflections of my own journey. These lessons about friendships, boundaries, and personal growth are subjective, drawn from my unique path. They might not resonate with everyone, and that's perfectly fine. Everyone's journey is different, and what works for me may not work for you. Friendships are deeply personal, and the way we navigate them can vary greatly depending on who we are and where we are in life. What's important is that we stay open to the lessons each relationship offers, and we take what resonates with us, leaving behind what doesn't. The balance between forming connections with others and maintaining our true selves is something I'm still learning to embrace. And for that, I owe so much to Ala, who taught me that staying true to who you are is one of the most important things you can do in any relationship.

Take your time to figure out what works best for you. Reflect on the dynamics of your relationships, understand the nature of the people you interact with, and develop alibis that feel authentic and effective. It's a process, and there's no rush. If you find that any of the ideas or suggestions shared in this book resonate with you or help you in some way, I'd genuinely love to hear about it. Feel free to share your experiences with me. You can drop me a direct message on Instagram at **@gogoijoydeep**, and who knows? Your story might just inspire someone else on their journey to finding their own alibis.

So go on—start exploring, experimenting, and evolving. And remember, it's not about escaping responsibility but about communicating your boundaries and priorities in a way that feels right for you.

Bibliography

1. C. S. Lewis, *The Four Loves.*
2. Aristotle, *Nicomachean Ethics.*
3. John Thibaut & Harold Kelley, George Homans, and Peter Blau, *Social Exchange Theory.*
4. Dr. Henry Cloud, *Boundaries.*
5. Stephen Covey, *The 7 Habits of Highly Effective People.*
6. Melody Beattie, *Codependent No More.*
7. Harriet Lerner, *The Dance of Anger.*
8. Brené Brown, *The Gifts of Imperfection.*
9. Jim Rohn, "We are the average of the five people we spend the most time with." (Popular Quote).
10. Helen Keller, "Walking with a friend in the dark is better than walking alone in the light." (Popular Quote).
11. Aristotle, "Wishing to be friends is quick work, but friendship is a slow ripening fruit." (Popular Quote).

Although I have mentioned the crux of the books above, for those seeking further insights into the complexities of relationships and personal development, I highly recommend these works as companions to this book.

Final Thought

Friendship, at its best, is both a mirror and a refuge—a reflection of who we are and a safe haven where we can grow. If this book has sparked even a small moment of reflection or clarity in your life, then my purpose has been fulfilled. Thank you for allowing me to be a part of your journey, and you can share your experience directly on my Instagram: @gogoijoydeep.

www.ingramcontent.com/pod-product-compliance
Lightning Source LLC
LaVergne TN
LVHW091053150826
845673LV00002B/566

* 9 7 9 8 8 9 6 7 3 8 7 0 1 *